To Roy & Julia

PL's

D0265179

A SPOON
WITH EVERY COURSE

A
SPOON
WITH
EVERY
COURSE

In Search of the
Legendary Food of France

MIRABEL OSLER

Illustrations by
SIMON DORRELL
Recipes interpreted by SHAUN HILL

Mirabel Osler

PAVILION

First published in Great Britain in 1996 by
PAVILION BOOKS LIMITED
26 Upper Ground, London SE1 9PD

Text copyright © Mirabel Osler 1996
Illustrations copyright © Simon Dorrell 1996
Interpretation of recipes copyright © Shaun Hill 1996

A CIP catalogue record for this book is available from the British Library

ISBN 1 85793 766 X

Typeset in 9½ on 14pt Walbaum Roman and Garamond Italics
Printed and bound in Finland by W.S.O.Y.

2 4 6 8 10 9 7 5 3 1

This book may be ordered by post direct from the publisher.
Please contact the Marketing Department.
But try your bookshop first.

Contents

BY THE SAME AUTHOR

A Gentle Plea for Chaos
The Garden Bench
The Garden Wall
The Secret Gardens of France
In the Eye of the Garden

ACKNOWLEDGEMENTS

I WOULD LIKE TO THANK the following people for giving me help and advice: Delphine Alliod, Michel Arnalot, Phillipe Arnaud, Claire Brentnall, Christian Dallemagne, Shaun Hill, Colin Hingston, Clare Kirkman, Lesley Mackley, Odile Masquelier, Paul Mitchell, John and Pauline Napper, Sigrid Neville, Sir Roy Strong, Dr Katherine Swift and Dr Julia Trevelyan Oman. In particular I would like to thank Diana Voos, who gave me so much invaluable help in the Ardèche, and Prue Bellak and Ken Swift for trying out recipes.

Finally Tamsin, not only for her translating and transcribing, but for her enthusiasm, her willingness to go anywhere, taste anything, and to have a positive outlook towards any situation, however unpromising it appeared.

NOTES ABOUT THE RECIPES

BECAUSE COOKING IS AN IMPRECISE ART, it's almost impossible for weights and measures or oven temperatures to be set in stone. I've included a few recipes at the end of each chapter, more or less as they were given to me, but skilfully adapted by Shaun Hill for those of you who would like to try them. Accuracy doesn't come into it but improvization, gastronomic intuition and your sense of smell, feel and taste do. The weather or time of year, or the age and freshness of ingredients may be critical to whether a recipe works or not, but even so no dish turns out the same every time, despite the fact that the ingredients are identical. Some of the recipes are simple, others sound wildly unattainable. Using basil because you can't get your hands on dill may change the mood of the course but will not detract from the result.

Shaun Hill told me to distrust all recipes, and in particular those given to me by chefs! Chefs cook from a totally different base from that used in a domestic kitchen. A chef, before he or she starts, will have little bowls – the *mise en place* of chopped shallots, herbs, mushrooms, etc, in place. He scoops up handfuls of ingredients for each dish he cooks, never weighing or measuring a thing, whether it's butter, chopped ginger, wine or cream.

Chapter 1

THE
ORIGIN
OF
THE QUEST

Chartreuse

Chapter I
Chartreuse

The Origin of the Quest

Among the autumn crocus sprinkling the upland meadows of the Chartreuse, Honorine, Clotilde's grandmother, grazed her three cows. By the time the first bitter winds from the east reached the pasture, and before the snow weighed down the branches of the chestnuts, Honorine would bring the cattle down to the valley. The sound of their bells, each chime at variance with the other, is one of Clotilde's first memories. More than sixty years ago, accompanying her grandmother, she would loiter among the leaves searching for *girolles* or for hazelnuts within her reach. That was before she was old enough to be put to work: to pump water and scrub the pails; to feed chickens and clean out the rabbits; it was before she was responsible for helping her mother make cheese from a mixture of goats' and cows' milk, or was able to handle the small knife used for preparing vegetables in the kitchen.

To find this area you must forsake the autoroute south of Chambéry and take the more northern N6, which winds south-west towards Grenoble, and travel through the small valleys, gorges and cols where the Granier mountain reaches the height of 1,938 metres and where monks made the famed liqueur, Grande-Chartreuse, from a distillation of herbs.

Chez Clotilde
Was There a Summer?

The first time my husband Michael and I met Clotilde was late one afternoon when we went to enquire about an evening meal. A stag's head hung over the door of the dining-room and against one wall stood an old pianola untouched, Clotilde told us later, since her father had last played it. In the darkening kitchen, moving heavily with a limp caused by arthritis and speaking in a slightly husky voice, as though her vocal chords had been smoked over juniper as constantly as the joints that hung around the chimney, Clotilde offered us small glasses of *marc* made from her apples. Having a few moments to herself, she responded to our questions: yes, she had

always lived in this region; she remembered both her mother and grandmother sharing the cooking, depending on who had gone to market, who was turning the hay or plucking a fowl. A soup pot stood permanently on the range; in winter it was cabbage soup, well seasoned and with pieces of finely-chopped smoked bacon, to be eaten with chunks of *pain de campagne*, huge round boulders that last so well. And she remembers cleaning the crock, before brine was added, in which to preserve joints of meat, or salting a belly of pork for *petit salé*. In those days sugar was a luxury; they used instead their own honey for sweetening. And from an early age the children were taught which edible berries and wild herbs to bring to the kitchen.

We would have liked to linger, asking questions about her child-hood, the restaurant and how she managed now as an old lady, but there always seemed to be someone delivering a basket of mush-rooms, bags of groceries, paraffin, and something that looked very much like candles. They were. We learnt later how precarious the electricity was in a thunderstorm or if too great a load was put on the supply. When an old man arrived with a couple of dead hares in a sack and it was obvious some haggling was about to take place, we left. Clotilde's parting words to us were, 'You must come back. Come in three days! Then you shall taste my roast hare with beetroot.' Since those carefree days, strict laws now forbid this kind of hunting and barter. Even so a certain phlegmatic attitude means that victims of *la chasse* are still on the menu, even if this involves a few back-handers and surreptitious bargaining with those in uniform.

That was our first encounter with Chez Clotilde – an occasion to be followed by many others as we travelled through France on our way to Italy and Greece. Once, sitting on a bench in the pallid April sunlight when the snow still lay across the mountain peaks, and the stream that flowed into the turbulent Cozon was the colour of milk, Clotilde spoke about herself. All around us, in spite of the annual slaughter that takes place throughout France of everything from a lark to a nightingale, birds sang with such spirited vitality we almost expected to see their notes penetrating the upper air. Wearing a purple woolly cap over her wispy grey hair and pausing for a while from her morning chores, Clotilde became quite garrulous as she related rambling stories of her family. I tried to unravel the legends. There was an Aunt Solange, who went to the bad; Uncle Prosper, who had made money from tinkering; cousin Crépin, who was a bit simple, and a whole galaxy of nephews and nieces with shining names such as Tatiana, Edwige, Sabine and Sylvestre (he must have become a forester, surely?) who had each, in one way or another, been affected by the existence of the restaurant, Chez Clotilde.

It has always been known as Chez Clotilde. Ask her, and she will tell you she never remembers a moment when the name was deliberately chosen. Rather it evolved. After she was widowed in her early twenties when her husband, Apollinaire, had been killed in a hunting accident, she started to serve meals as a means of augmenting her livelihood. Her parents had died in the war and Clotilde, now head of the family, had a brother, Gaspar, and two sisters, Angèle and Modeste, to support. I commented on the family's uncommon names. 'My *grand-maman* was most devout,' she said touching a cross that hung on a chain round her neck. 'Ah, Honorine! She insisted on us all being named after our appropriate feast days.' She smiled and added, 'My parents could not possibly disobey!' She brought out old photographs of earlier years – dim, slightly out of focus and smelling of mould from the dresser drawer; it was possible to make out Clotilde as a dark-haired figure, strong and upright.

As a young widow, renowned for her generous cooking, it wasn't long before those in need of fortification on a cold day took to dropping in for a bowl of leek and potato soup as dense and rough as a blanket, or for a helping of savoury pigeon stew augmented with lumps of salted pork. Anyone and everyone – the travelling blacksmith, the schoolmaster, chimney-sweep, the curate or a carpenter; hunters, itinerant pedlars and, occasionally, a wandering functionary – all found their way to Clotilde's table, which at that time was a massive piece of wood eight inches deep and scoured from generations of jointing venison and wild boar. It stood in the centre of her kitchen. At one end was a range fired by wood, at the other a hearth where a black cauldron was suspended from a *crémaillère*, an iron arm, in which *lentilles au petit salé* could be left simmering for hours or where a tripod straddled the embers for grilled fish, joints of poultry and meat or sausages. The hiss of spitting fat falling on to logs filled the room and blue smoke lingered round the rafters.

The smell of good food travels as rapidly as gossip. Soon Clotilde needed a second long table; she set out a modest price list, and as her menus became extended, more members of her family were drawn in to help with the ducks, beehives, milking the ewes and goats, cheese making and seeing to the cellar – the light Apremont from the Alpine slopes of Chambéry or Chignin from vineyards south of Seyssel. Brother-in-law Patrice, a little erratic with his rod and gun, would dump fish or game on the kitchen table; other members of the family cut and split logs, slaughtered rabbits, poultry and pigs, dug the potager for turnips, carrots and a fleshier kind of sorrel which, along with the wild one, Clotilde used in dozens of traditional ways such as a tenderly green soup thickened with egg yolks. There were pumpkins, cauliflowers, celeriac and a choice of potatoes, including *ratte* or *quenelles de Lyon*, so versatile that it's madness we don't grow them in Britain.

In the beginning nothing was written down, but any traveller could be sure by midday of finding an earthenware pot of *terrine de lapin* made from wild rabbit, nuts, fatty pork and a liberal dose of *eau-de-vie* on the table, or a plate of sliced ham and a tall jar alongside full of gherkins pickled with sprigs of thyme and a crumbling of bay leaves and always, ready to be put together on the instant, there was that once ubiquitous but delicious dish that alas is seldom found nowadays, *oeufs mayonnaise*. And when her brother Gaspar returned home after a successful fishing expedition, *truite au bleu* served with butter was on the menu; or better still, when there was a pike, with its long head and small scales lying at the bottom of his fishing basket, *quenelles de brochet* (which Clotilde always shaped by hand) drew to her table those enthusiasts for their delicacy of flavour. The *quenelles* were nothing like the tasteless lumps of fishy flour you get nowadays where the chef has been economical with the truth.

Gratin dauphinois, whenever we had it, was cooked in a shallow dish with such a crusty top it hid the sizzling and garlicky blend of potatoes and cream underneath. Radishes, peas, broad beans and salads were some of the vegetables that appeared in their seasonal order. Puréed spinach, bulked out with cream sauce, was often there in such large quantities that it was assumed everyone would help themselves to at least two servings as the huge white bowl was passed around the table.

It wasn't long, Clotilde explained as she peeled apples for *beignets de pommes*, before she added three more tables in an adjoining room to the kitchen and wrote out the daily menu on a slate; Sundays were a family occasion when wives and children joined in the serious eating, which lasted late into the afternoon. (As any traveller in France knows, when they find a paucity of choice on the Sunday evening menu and the cook is looking frazzled, they can be sure the restaurant is a good one.)

Chez Clotilde has never become trendy. Nothing is likely to change while she is in charge. Despising a tendency for fast food and gadgets, she sticks to the traditions she learnt as a child. What is in season will appear on her table. Olives, anchovies (sold loose, not in tins), spices, capers, pulses, and so on are all available in local markets; but what makes Clotilde's restaurant stand way above many indifferent places you now find in France is that most of what you eat, if it doesn't come from her immediate locality, is either produced on her land, or gathered wild from the surrounding terrain. Her methods are slow and old-fashioned. She showed us a tinned copper *daubière* for braising beef in red-wine stock; a primitive iron *salamandre* with a long handle for heating on the fire before caramelizing sugar; there were various old *marmites*, *cocottes*, tureens and ramekins; smooth-handled kitchen knives, their blades thin as shavings, and a row of sieves hanging from the wall with their flimsy mesh worn to cobwebs.

THE LAST TIME WE WENT to Clotilde's, turning up the narrow valley road, it was autumn. How the appetite quivers on the threshold of her kitchen. The distinct smell of good butter heating in a pan and of garlic roasting in the oven intermingled with the homely trace of damp ironing as Angèle hurriedly pressed the napkins before lunch, enveloped us in an atmosphere redolent of promises. The menu, as usual, was reassuringly short but even so choice was critical: chestnut soup or cheese soufflé concealing poached eggs; *andouillettes*, *écrevisses* cooked over the fire or roast lamb with juniper berries; *fromage de chèvre*, *St Marcellin* and *fromage de brebis* (made from ewe's milk) followed by *tarte aux myrtilles*.

Against a background of bubbling and gurgling, of the scoop of ladle in a tureen, of murmuring from the kitchen and guttural sighs surrounding us, we spent three hours of contentment and indulgence. Not until our plates were pushed aside and half-empty glasses abandoned, did the thought of black coffee offer us the only hope of not succumbing to the soporific warmth and the comforting balm of a perfect meal.

But how much longer can this last? Will her restaurant be bought up, her reputation for good food adding noughts to the price as the place is pulled apart, to re-emerge with shiny brown and orange décor, plastic sconces and fake logs in the fireplace? Outside, in a gold frame, will an implausibly long menu only be changed when the paper starts to curl? Please not. Please don't let this happen. Let the door be locked, the sign taken down and the chalk of the last menu stealthily be blurred by dust. Better by far that the restaurant goes with her; that the cotton napkins grow mouldy in the dresser along with the photograph of Clotilde as a young woman. Let nothing remain except for a trace of green walnuts and outside, on summer evenings, a sweet scent of clover.

FOR YEARS IN FRANCE there used to be restaurants on the fringes of cities, in towns, or standing isolated in the countryside, where outside stood a wooden outline of a chef (or worse, a pig) with the day's menu pinned to his distended stomach. The more vehicles with French, not foreign, number plates parked outside, the more the traveller could depend on the meal being good. But no longer; for alas, a table ready laid with heavy cotton napkins, a carafe of wine, a basket of bread and the cruet, a massive contraption that included both olive oil and vinegar, have long ago left the small, lunchtime restaurants of France.

And so deprived I felt at this loss, so disheartened by the tendency for elaborate menus of obviously microwaved food, that when the artist Simon Dorrell suggested we search for the Clotildes and others of the culinary world to see if they still existed, I felt fired by enthusiasm to take on the quest. It turned out, at times, to be more uphill than I had expected, but like the months I spent a few years ago digging out material for my book *The Secret Gardens of France*, the country is full of unforeseen paradoxes. There are no infallible guidelines.

If you find a kind of relentless negativity in this chapter, it's only because when I started out I met with a certain cynical detachment from Francophiles who had become disenchanted.

Frederic Raphael, in an article 'Why Is It that You Just Can't Get a Decent Meal in France These Days?' (published in the *Daily Mail*, October 1994) writes: 'Gastronomy is turning from an art into just one more form of marketing . . . Little by little, the great tradition has become the great con.' Compare his words to those of Freda White, written forty years ago: 'French cookery, French wine, are not only unsurpassed; they are supreme . . . Naturally the cook makes his *plat du jour* of the best the morning market has to offer.' Naturally? Oh, naturally no longer. An ever-widening chasm lies between the two writers.

Had I read Raphael's words before I launched myself into French kitchens I might never have started. And yet, and yet – what a lot I would have missed. I know it was hard work and, at times, remorselessly disheartening as day after day we found restaurants of unmitigated nastiness; restaurants where the production had nothing to do with appetite, felicity, gratification, satiety, indulgence or even Epicurus. Boil-in-the-bag hollandaise sauce is not exactly a turn-on. And the trouble is, unlike researching French gardens when I could retreat from duds unscathed and visit a different garden, once launched into a meal we were doomed to walk the plank. Nor could we manage another three- or four-course meal, varied enough to do the chef justice, for the next twenty-four hours. At least I couldn't. Nor could Simon. In the end we missed out breakfast altogether as we prepared ourselves for the next lunchtime onslaught. I know this sounds pitiful, but two main meals a day – day after day – was not usually how we lived our lives at home, and you have to work hard to find a restaurant where you say on leaving: 'We will return.'

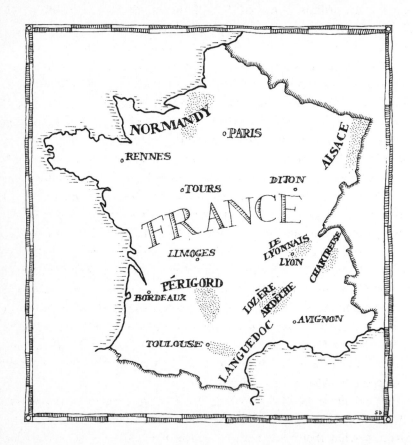

BESIDES SIMON, another companion on some of my journeys was David Wheeler, proprietor and publisher of the gardening quarterly *Hortus*, and of *Convivium – The Journal of Good Eating*. We worked well together. I'm not at ease unearthing facts and figures; in gardens I dodge the Latin. I prefer to free-fall into a situation and record what I see, feel, sense and smell, but David, who writes articles on prescribed subjects and number of words, needs facts. Travelling together we complemented each other in our approach to what we found. He is the professional, questioning and searching for data; I prefer to be a canary taken down the mine to see if I keel over when the air is lethal.

Our self-imposed brief was to find out if, as Freda White once so innocently promised in those far-off halcyon days, 'The traveller will find himself astonished at the meals he will eat in little inns, and tiny cafés – if luck guides him.' We wanted to discover if there were still cooks who changed their menus more often than twice a year; those who were predominantly regional or others who grew their own produce. What were the chef's own feelings on tradition and diversity? What childhood memories of the family cuisine did they have, and what did they think about the ebb and flow of fashionable fads in the kitchen that have been so radical in the last twenty years?

Would we find restaurants that catered for a dependable local clientèle, as opposed to transitory tourists, as well as for those serious eaters – seemingly immortal – the travelling salesmen who keep up a lively network of information linking the whole of the country as to where reasonably priced and delicious food can still be found? 'I know from long experience that French commercial travellers delight in good food and have a real genius for discovering it,' wrote an Englishman in 1950. In 1994 a hotelier told us that *Les hommes d'affaires* (what a happy title) now cut down on their travelling by compressing their visits to clients. 'Look!' he waved to his almost deserted dining-room, 'here we offer a menu *gastronomique* – two doors down at the pizzeria, they are full!'

Would there be chefs who, like the great Fernand Point at the Restaurant de la Pyramide, Vienne – he died in 1955 – plan their meals around what they find that day in the market, who buy only what looks fresh, and what is in season? The celebrated masters of cooking today have passed down Fernand Point's digestive system whose simple dictum was: 'Every morning one begins again from zero, with nothing on the stoves. That is cuisine.' If only it were still so everywhere. Nowadays Point could easily find nothing on the stoves each morning because everything is in the freezer.

One of those celebrated masters of cooking, Paul Bocuse in the Lyonnais, never decides beforehand what will be on the day's cheapest menu until he goes to market. If pike looks good it will appear on the table along with whatever fresh and dewy vegetables he finds; the ripest and sweetest of fruit, and cheese at the peak of its maturity. Whereas another renowned chef, Alain Chapel, only twenty-odd kilometres from Lyon who, in his youth, was inspired by Fernand Point, does the reverse. Once he's found producers who can supply him with the very best, he depends on them utterly. He goes to one for his pullets, another for cherries, another for dairy produce and so on. But, like the Bernard family at l'Aigle (see page 99), he is always on the lookout for new sources. This keeps the menu from going stale and the chef from becoming atrophied. Nothing is more disheartening than to find a good restaurant where the food is excellent but when you return the menu hasn't changed a jot, not even on the *plat du jour* when 'today's special' is the same as yesterday's; the same as last month's. This is no exaggeration, I do know of such places. The predictability of a too familiar choice takes away anticipation.

As with gardens, you need to be confounded.

Les Halles, the famous and lively market starting at 3.00 am, had been in the centre of Paris for a century. Here late revellers, having dined in elegant restaurants, went 'slumming' in the dives surrounding the market, where there was everything from grilled lobsters to stuffed mushrooms, woodcock cooked with champagne to fishballs. Dancing and breakfasting on tripe (which could be taken away in an earthenware jar) before going home, the diners would sidestep carts being trundled through the city streets packed high with green-plumed vegetables, glossy onions and the sculptured perfection of artichokes. In old photographs of the fish market the saleswomen are wearing heavy black dresses and white bonnets tied under their chins. Les Halles was uprooted in 1969 to Rungis, on the outskirts near Orly airport, to much lamentation and nostalgic hand-wringing but to the greater advantage of far-flung chefs. Would we find cooks, hundreds of miles away, who ordered their produce regularly from Rungis market? 'A marvellous – and dreadful – place,' according to Jane Grigson, 'the grandest and most important market in, and for, Europe . . . '

To get me in the mood, I read some of my diaries of French journeys which Michael and I had made forty or more years ago. We were transformed by discovering France after the war, so when Elizabeth David's *French Provincial Cooking* appeared in 1960, I went right through the book noting down every single name and the whereabouts (if I could trace them) of restaurants where she had eaten dishes that she describes so eloquently:

> An onion tart, flat as a plate but still somehow oozing with cream, preceded a subtly flavoured sausage served hot with a mild and creamy horseradish sauce as the only accompaniment, followed by *haricots verts* fairly saturated in butter; we were then beguiled into eating a sweet called a *vacherin glacé*. This turned out to be an awe-inspiring confection of ice-cream, glacé fruits, frozen whipped cream, and meringue, that left me temporarily speechless.

Luckily for the rest of us, not for long.

There are few nostalgic pains so acute as those we undergo when looking back at old travelling itineraries. The vast structure of recollection is reassembled layer upon layer. That which took weeks to live through, with an intensity we only experience when lifted out of context, is reawakened by retracing routes across a map. We chip away at the memory for something just beyond recall: a certain sight, or smell, or taste. My eldest daughter, who has no need to write down menus, remembers every good meal she's eaten abroad, but for me – like gardeners who go to bed with plant lists – I loll about reading accounts of what feasts we ate years ago. I read my old travelling notes knowing I shall end by sighing. France. The country we turned to for civilized living.

My resolution almost faltered when, on the first of our journeys, I saw a French car ahead of us waiting to board the ferry to Calais, loaded to the roof with packets of sliced white bread. What hope is left for the French to sustain their culinary standards when they themselves take factory bread, as pulpy as cottonwool, back to their kitchens? Fortunately those people are an aberration, a minority, for all over France there are still bakers so concerned with traditionally baked bread that tastes, smells and feels good, that they retain their ovens fuelled by wood. One such place in the centre of Lyon appears later in the book.

When you've had a bad meal and the chef admits to having gone to a catering rather than a cooking school, you can understand why everything seemed wrong, including the muzak – which is still rare in French restaurants. At a restaurant in the Ardèche the over-sized plates of magenta, heliotrope and black on which slices of brown duck curled at the edges and the chocolate on the *profiteroles* was economically pallid, proved my point. No wonder many of us have become disenchanted with food in France. This feeling was compounded at the outset. Up until this year we'd always found that a handwritten menu outside a restaurant, *brasserie* or Café de Commerce guaranteed an inexpensive but reasonable and un-pretentious lunch. Generations of travellers had depended on such places (as they did with Routiers spread across the *routes nationales*) for reliable, homely cooking. So, seeing a small restaurant on a village square in the Rhône valley with a notice pinned to the windowsill for a sixty-franc, four-course menu written in red biro, and inside long tables laid with bread and bottles of red wine, I persuaded Simon and David that we could be assured of getting a good meal. With luck it might be exceptionally good.

I had to eat my words. (If only that was all I'd done.) In no time the restaurant had filled up with *habitués,* workers from the near-by nuclear plant, who obviously put up with the most atrocious, utterly inedible stuff that ever passed for food. The occasion was only redeemed for us by the waitress. She was smiling and friendly: a tall girl with a long mass of dark curly hair wearing a divided skirt and a low-cut singlet under a half-buttoned shirt. She leant across an empty chair to recite the menu, looking more like a wet-nurse than a waitress – her bosomy opulence was the only generous ingredient in the place. We were each given a plate with a slice of pudenda-pink spam decorated with two gherkins and an olive on it; this was followed by guinea-fowl stew sloshing in brown swill and a ratatouille where water had replaced olive oil. But what makes this place memorable were our simultaneous gasps of disbelief at the third course, the cheese. Three morsels, no bigger than postage stamps, were stuck to the plates set before us. David's plate was still warm from the sink so that whatever their origins, the scraps melted into a homogeneous goo before his eyes. Nowhere ever, however humble the meal in France, have I seen cheese served in this way. If there is only one kind, the cheese is at least brought to the table to be sliced according to your appetite. Sour wine only endorsed the experience so that by the time the wet-nurse offered ice-cream or *crème caramel* our gullets were in spasm.

By going to the restaurant I had, with unwavering but misplaced reasoning, chosen the worst place I've eaten in for years. My disillusionment was assuaged somewhat when two days later in the Ardèche, we lunched among market traders on *salade de fruits de mer* or *charcuterie de pays*; *andouillette à la moutarde* or grilled steak, cheese and dessert.

For the traveller who uses a guidebook, there are no absolute certainties. Even as you read, the information may be out of date. It's a protracted journey from the source of the material to the day the guide appears on bookshop shelves. Not only may prices have gone up, but the chef may have changed, the category be misleading; and if you rely on the plethora of plaques stuck on the hotel wall, beware!

At more than one restaurant we found that on *Le Bottin Gourmand* plaque, the year of the award had been scratched out. Only by careful scrutiny at one place could we make out the ghostly figures. They were six years out of date and the hotel had not been evaluated since.

One-starred restaurants can usually be relied on, but two-stars can be dodgy. The rating may have a bias towards décor, ambience, presentation and size, or to the length of the menu rather than the chef's integrity. In the *Michelin Guide* it's important to note the grade of the establishment as well as its star quality. For instance, a two-spoon-and-fork restaurant with only one star, such as Au Déjeuner de Sousceyrac (see page 70), can be well worth a detour. The money has gone into the kitchen and the ingredients, not the light fittings. Even so, there are listed places which should know better than to serve soup with *croûtons* from a packet looking like miniature dog biscuits in place of fresh *croûtons* fried in butter. And where are the vegetables? Why, even in starred restaurants, is there a paucity of the produce that grows in lush swathes in potagers, or weighs down market stalls with young, succulent promise? Who buys them, these delicious-looking vegetables? Not chefs, apparently. Or not enough of them. Once upon a time vegetables used to be served as an indispensable course in every meal.

Taking advice about where to eat is as risky as taking advice as to what to plant in your garden. Until you've seen what your informant chooses – in the garden or the restaurant – you can't be sure that it isn't just theatrical presentation that turns them on. I have planted some virulent horrors on the advice of tip-top gardeners; and, as for eating, heavens! It was only on rare occasions that we had the sagacity to back out of recommended places with suspiciously long menus, or in which waiters in tapestry waistcoats hovered on the threshold against a background of empty tables. When you look for a restaurant, what comes first? Accessibility or expense? The ambience or the food? I've no doubt in my mind, it has to be the food, whether the place has a dirt floor or lurid grandeur, whether it's functional or full of graceless tat.

One of my most helpful informants told me that it's only among the peasants that the old culinary skills are maintained. 'You have no *paysans* left in England, but we do in France. It's they who still pass down the traditional art of cooking and preserving to their daughters.' As the seasons come round, so these countrywomen preserve prunes, dry strings of rosy garlic under the eaves, make greengage *eau-de-vie* and jars of tomato sauce. These are accomplishments they learnt from their mothers and grandmothers so that they grew up knowing how to do their own curing (*salaison*) from the family pig, how to make *confits* (meat preserved in fat) and to stretch filo pastry until it became as pliant as fine chamois leather – a feat that requires such dexterity it cannot be learnt from a book.

'Modern housewives who nowadays often have jobs', I was told, 'have no time for this sort of cuisine. You have to go into the agricultural areas of France, to the villages and to the farms, to discover the true regional fare.' But sadly, if the perpetuation of good cooking depends on the young of France and if they no longer learn the basic skills, or are preoccupied, indifferent or put up instead with 'le fast food', then what hope for a culinary future? As John Ardagh found out during his mammoth research for his book on France in the 1980s, *France Today*:

> The French, at least in the middle classes, used to eat serenely well as a matter of course every day, especially in their homes. But a modern nation in a hurry no longer has such time or concern for serious daily cooking and eating . . . And ordinary restaurants, faced with soaring costs, have been cutting corners, using mass-production techniques and second-rate processed foods, and their clients accept it.

As we travelled, meeting cooks, market shoppers and traders, it became clear how prophetic those words were. Only the elderly appear to be cooking at home. And as this is happening throughout Europe it seems an inexorable movement and one we have to accept, but one we should lament because, of all countries, France has so much to lose. Fortunately, in the restaurant world, there are chefs who fight like tigers for the integrity of their cuisines; their restaurants become famed, proving that there still exists a clientèle willing to travel far and to pay whatever it costs to eat well.

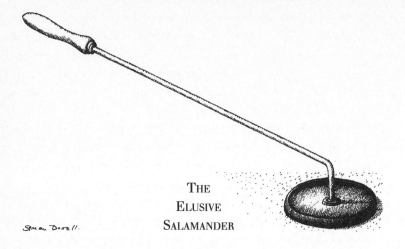

THE
ELUSIVE
SALAMANDER

Salamander . . . a mythical fire-breathing monster and thus the
name of an iron implement which can be made red hot in the
coals of an open fire.

PRIMARILY THE INCENTIVE for the venture belongs wholly to Clotilde, that inspirational figure who appears at the beginning of the book – not only for my memories of Chez Clotilde but because it was in her kitchen that I first saw that ancient tool, the salamander, whose use goes back beyond the Middle Ages. In 1769 it was described as a 'circular iron plate that is heated and placed over a pudding or other dish to brown it'. Nothing has changed in the last 200 years. Elizabeth David's definition of a salamander is 'A round iron utensil with a long handle, also called a *fer à glacer* and a *pelle rouge*. The iron is made red hot and held close to the surface of a dish the top of which is by this means instantaneously browned, without the possibility of the main body of the dish being overheated and therefore altering in any way in consistency.' I felt my search was grounded when I read her next words. 'These utensils are now all but obsolete, at any rate in England, and so far as I know nothing has yet been devised to replace them in the domestic kitchen.'

Salamanders are all but obsolete in France, too. And just as we saw an ingenious *souvlakia* trader in a market square in the Peloponnese using his wife's hair-dryer to liven up the charcoal, so nowadays innovative cooks get round the absence of salamanders by using a blow torch for their *gratins* or *crèmes brûlées*. But I wanted a salamander. I wanted to hold that heavy object with its long, well-balanced handle; I wanted one to live beside the fire to use whenever anything needed a shot of bracing treatment such as white of eggs when they wouldn't set in an *oeufs au gratin*.

The story of my search for chefs and salamanders is personal and unstructured. The regions we went to are arbitrary; they don't hang together consecutively with regard to season and geography, rather I have arranged them in the way I felt they contrasted one to the other. France is such a vast country we could only cover small areas in short bursts. Hundreds of restaurants, no doubt with greater merit than those we visited, exist all over the country. The variety of places in the book ranges from a *winstub*, a mountain *auberge*, to one- or two-starred restaurants, but germane to their inclusion is whether we ate well there or not. Altogether I write about only a handful; some already well known, others so far unrecorded. Some came to us through chefs themselves or those gourmets who were willing to share their knowledge with us, and when everything else failed we pored over countless menus outside restaurants – rejecting most – or we followed our noses by blundering about among the clammy scent of fungi, or relying on the promise of a good meal in a leguminous locality.

It may take some searching to find a restaurant to which you would like to return. But don't be put off. In the succeeding chapters are accounts of quite superb chefs and their restaurants; of cooks enthusiastic and positive, young and upbeat, who believe in the future, believe in their cuisine and believe that they are moving in the right direction. Nothing I experienced, even in our worst moments, will put me off returning again and again to France. The fact that one has to persevere to find good eating in no way takes away from the great diversity of epicurean pleasure to be found on the other side of the Channel.

The book is intended as a celebration of France, a reassurance to those who have travelled through and loved the country that other Chez Clotildes do exist, and that with stubborn tenacity and a belief in the culinary heritage of France, we shall still be able to find what Marcel Boulestin wrote about long ago: 'recipes of quite remarkable local dishes, handed down, like Homer's verses, from generation to generation . . . '

RECIPES

ASK CLOTILDE FOR RECIPES and you'll find it as impossible as gathering dew to fill the kettle. She is imprecise. No weights, no measures, merely an instinctive feel for what goes with what based on family cooking imbibed since childhood. How can she say what temperature the oven should be when it's a matter of piling on the wood or cooking over embers? Instead I suggest you practise her method. Stick a finger into everything and taste. She pricks, nibbles and pokes until she is satisfied that every dish can be brought to the table.

POTAGE DES PETITS POIS
FRESH PEA SOUP

SERVES 4-6

100 g/4 oz/½ cup unsalted butter
800 g/1¾ lb young shelled peas
1 litre/1¾ pt/4¼ cups chicken stock
2 tbsp chervil leaves
salt and pepper

ELT THE BUTTER IN A PAN. Add the peas, cover and cook gently for a few minutes. Add the stock and cook until tender, about 8–10 minutes. Remove a heaped tablespoonful of peas and set aside to garnish the finished dish.

Rub the peas through a sieve or liquidize in a blender. Return to the pan and reheat, adding the spoonful of peas, some leaves of chervil and salt and pepper. If the soup is a little too thick, add more stock.

POCHOUSE
FRESHWATER FISH STEW

HIS IS A KIND OF MATELOTE – a fish stew using white or red wine – made of freshwater fish. Clotilde's *pochouse* is dependent on eel to which she adds perch, carp and tench in equal proportions.

SERVES 8
25 g/1 oz/2 tbsp butter
100 g/4 oz unsmoked streaky bacon, cut into 1 cm/½ in cubes
2 medium carrots, peeled and sliced
3 medium onions, peeled and sliced
12 pickling onions
1.8 kg/4 lb freshwater fish, such as eel, carp, tench, perch
2 cloves garlic, crushed
50 ml/2 fl oz/¼ cup dry white wine
bouquet garni
40 g/1½ oz/3 tbsp unsalted butter
40 g/1½ oz/6 tbsp plain (all-purpose) flour
cream for serving

ELT THE BUTTER IN A LARGE PAN and fry the bacon, carrots and both kinds of onion until golden.

Add the fish, garlic, wine and *bouquet garni*. Cover, bring to the boil and simmer for 20 minutes. Lift the fish and bacon into a tureen ready for serving.

Mix together the butter and flour to make *beurre manié*. Add the *beurre manié*, in pieces, to the pan off the heat to thicken the stew. Reheat to simmering point, then serve with cream.

TARTE TATIN

A TARTE TATIN is turned on its head so that the pastry covering is at the bottom. Clotilde used Cox's Orange Pippins. She cooks the *tarte* in a tin-lined skillet, 6 cm/2½ in deep.

SERVES 6-8

FOR THE PASTRY:

225 g/8 oz/1 cup unsalted butter, cut into 2.5 cm/1 in cubes

300 g/11 oz/2¾ cups plain (all-purpose) flour

1 egg

FOR THE FILLING:

200 g/7 oz/⅞ cup sugar

100 g/4 oz/½ cup unsalted butter

6 medium apples, Cox's or Granny Smiths, peeled, cored and cut into segments

MIX THE CUBES OF BUTTER into the flour. Add the egg and 100 ml/4 fl oz/½ cup water, and mix to a dough. Roll out as if making puff pastry, leaving the butter cubes intact, into a rectangle, then mark and fold into three. Rest the dough in the refrigerator for 30 minutes. Repeat the exercise three times.

Heat the oven to 190°C/375°F/Gas Mark 5. Melt the sugar in an ovenproof skillet, then heat until caramelized. Mix in the butter, then the apple segments.

Thinly roll out the pastry and cover the skillet. Bake for 30 minutes or until the pastry is golden. Turn upside down onto a plate and serve immediately.

Chapter II

DE
BOUCHE
A OREILLE

Lyonnais

Chapter II
Lyonnais
De Bouche à Oreille

FRANCE IN APRIL was a land of delicate colours. In a market were frilly leafed endives, *pissenlit* and sorrel; knuckle-shaped shallots and plump white asparagus, piled next to a pyramid of globe artichokes, lay alongside boxes of pale blue pansies under a row of men's caps hanging on meat hooks. The houses, painted the colour of the flesh of melons, had their grey shutters wide open to the spring light and in gardens neat circles of dwarf tulips formed mounded mauvish brassières enclosed by verbena and forget-me-nots. Poplars with leaves the colour of caramel lined the roads and further south a roundabout was filled with olive trees whose greyish-silver foliage was mimicked by cotton lavender spread beneath. Bluebells, cowslips and wood anemones, among saplings and wild cherries, added to the fragility of the countryside before fields of rape blasted off in a month's time. Even in Lyon the austerity of the riverside houses was softened by a blur of leaves from pollarded trees.

'*De bouche à oreille*' is the method recommended by Odile Masquelier for tracking down good restaurants. Odile and Georges live in Lyon, in a house overlooking the city. I'd first met them some years ago when I was researching for my book on the gardens of France, yet when I told her my new quest had nothing to do with gardens she rose to the challenge with her usual verve and enthusiasm. She, Georges and their friend Delphine offered to produce addresses for us, to make introductions, and to ply us with helpful advice. Odile kept her word and in the spring, forsaking her roses, she accompanied us down into the maelstrom of Lyon to lead us to a remarkable bakery and a restaurant we never would have found on our own.

Lyon, on the confluence of two rivers, is strategically placed in the heart of nourishing abundance. In each direction are sources of provender so diverse that it's no wonder the city is known as the capital of *la vraie cuisine française*, where the famous *saucissons de Lyon* can be found in most *charcuteries*, however remote. The Lyonnais stretches from the Bourgogne to the Ardèchc, from thc Auvergne to the Dauphiné. Lakes of freshwater fish, froggy meres and corn-fed *poulets de Bresse* are all near by. Lamb, pork and Charollais beef are part of the gastronomic landscape.

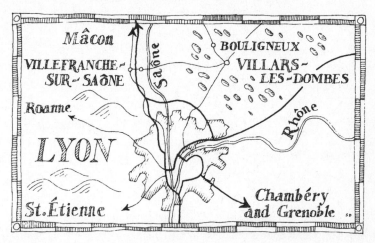

The surrounding fertility produces fruit and vegetables, truffles and *morilles*, as well as a whole tribe of cheeses. One, St Marcellin, we fruitlessly used to attempt to carry home. Alas, it never survived. Its creamy consistency, on the point of oozing, finally forced us to keep a special small basket in the car in which to convey the cheeses from market to dining table. Then there is *fromage blanc* which, when fresh, is unlike the passable but much more sterile factory-produced stuff now available in Britain. It appeared frequently on menus in the Lyonnais. Yet watching French diners ordering their cheese, we noticed how seldom anyone chose *fromage blanc* in lieu of the crusted Fourme Lyonnaise, the discs of Monts d'Or or the close-textured Pavé Dauphinois. But we did. A pile of *fromage blanc* smothered in thick cream (called *fraîche*, but tasting slightly off), the two sorts of white and the crunch of the sugar was irresistible. Coming from England the rich and fattening and guiltily self-indulgent bowlful was an alien alternative to Stilton or Cheddar.

Although we were in Lyon we didn't eat at the three-star Paul Bocuse a little out of the city. More modestly Odile took us to another Paul; the sort of restaurant you long to find everywhere, but without a French person to lead you by the hand only those with a truffle-hunting sort of nose will unearth such places for themselves.

Chez Paul
AN URBAN CLOTILDE

IN THE COMMERCIAL AREA of Lyon, in rue du Major-Martin – a little crack of a street – and opposite a hairdresser's called Odette, is the restaurant Chez Paul. A bar runs down one side of the room where men in berets were drinking among pots of lilies of the valley on the counter. (It was, after all, not far off the first of May when these flowers are symbolically handed around. At Marseille airport I was once given a bunch of them as I got off the plane.) One of the men was helping the overworked patron by pouring wine through a funnel into glass bottles or occasionally handing out the key to the lavatory that was a few doors down the street.

The rest of the room was jammed with five long tables, seating about forty altogether, laid with paper tablecloths and cotton napkins. In the corner stood a circular 'deer-horn' coat rack, but little else was allowed to take up space where another chair, if needed, could be fitted in.

At one table a group of men were mixing their own *kirs* from bottles of wine and *cassis* left on the table; some were talking, others silently eating or reading the newspaper. Brown jugs of wine stood on each table; the kind of jugs you see everywhere in France of such ugliness, both the colour and design, that they look as though white lard had trickled down the sides before setting solid. The wine turned out to be vigorous and unsophisticated, yet with none of that brutal acidity that can overwhelm the taste of food, however strident in flavour.

The proprietor was single-handed that day; usually his wife helped him, but as she was ill he was managing on his own. He did everything: cooking as well as serving at table. As the food was freshly cooked, apart from the salads he'd prepared beforehand, he was kept flying between kitchen and tables so that, although it wasn't a great area to traverse, he needed the agility of an acrobat. He dealt with orders, dishes, wine, bread, salads, coffee and bills at the same time as coping with cooking on two gas burners in a kitchen no larger than a ship's galley. Through blue smoke we could see fish and meat being cooked with the dexterity of a virtuoso.

There was no menu. As soon as we were seated, bread and a wedge of butter, cut like a slice from a cake with a black-handled knife left buried in its heart, were put on the table. First we were given that classic and, to the squeamish, unacceptable dish of *museau de boeuf* (ox muzzle), a traditional *hors d'oeuvre* still found ready-made in markets. Highly seasoned, the meat is sliced thinly and mixed with chopped herbs, shallots and marinated in vinaigrette dressing. But it was not our only *hors d'oeuvre*. There was a bowl of pickled herrings mixed in with chopped raw vegetables, another of dark green *lentilles du Puy* (crunchy – not mushy) with onions, oil and vinegar, and a bulky green salad dressed with walnut oil. We helped ourselves in turn, passing the big bowls one to another, from table to table.

Next came an earthenware pot of *rillettes*. I do love this stuff: it's a robust alternative to pâté and because it's loaded with fat it keeps well. In my enthusiastic youth I used to make it. Now I never do. I garden instead. Making *rillettes* is laborious; rather than pounding the goose, rabbit or pork in a mortar as is often prescribed in recipes, the meat should be shredded apart with two forks. It's the shredding that turns the ingredients into a tenderly fibrous texture. But only after several attempts did I get the seasoning right. If I was timid with the herbs, spices, salt and pepper we were left feeling internally stuck together from a surfeit of pig fat.

The main course was a choice of either sole, calves' liver or *entrecôte*. (When freshwater fish is on the menu it comes from the Jura or the Ain, where Paul visits a fisherman's inn to get fresh catches.) The sole was cooked in a shallow skillet in olive oil, while the *entrecôte* and liver were cooked in butter and arrived at table still spitting. Boiled potatoes coated in melting butter came in a separate dish. The activity, the freshness of the food, the penetrating flavours of cooking wafting out of the galley, mixed in with the smell from the smokers who, as everywhere in France, light up between courses whatever the rating of the restaurant, made us gradually slump into a pleasurable decline as the hours trickled away. It had to end sometime. And for the last course we were offered *fromage blanc* with a dish of cream alongside, a bowl of prunes laced with *eau-de-vie*, or one vast *crème caramel* floating in a dark amber sea and smelling of nursery puddings.

If this sounds like unrefined, basic fare, it was. But it was of the best and served in a way you seldom find any more: each dish self-contained, each separate, each left on the table for you to help yourself. With the tendency now to present food artily arranged on an arty plate, Chez Paul was memorable; if he hadn't been scuttling around in his effort to keep us all fed, I'd have liked to have asked him more about the restaurant. The bill, written on a piece of paper so faded at the edges it was obvious he was in the habit of presenting *l'addition* orally, came to 600 francs for five of us. And that included the wine and the coffee.

Having no *carte au restaurant* appeals to lots of people. It does to me. Ordering is simplified. You go in, and if the restaurant is reliable, you know you can depend on being served excellent food whatever is in the kitchen that day. But without a menu in the hand you do miss the anticipatory pleasure of reflecting over the possibilities while drinking an aperitif, discussing choices, and putting your own meal together.

As we walked away Odile murmured, 'Before it should be bad for me, it has to be good for me.' Not one of us contradicted her.

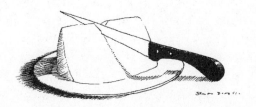

The Bakery
'This Bread I Break Was Once the Oat'

The smell on entering a bakery where the shop and the oven are in one room is as invigorating as the smell of roasting coffee. Maison de Confiance written across the window, with a sign above saying *Boulangerie Cuit au Bois*, are enough to quicken the pace of anyone interested in finding an alternative to that synthetic forgery we are usually compelled to eat for breakfast. Proust long ago anguished: had Françoise been dismissed, '. . . who would have baked me such hot rolls, made me such fragrant coffee . . . ?'

It might seem surprising to find in the hub of a city as large as Lyon a baker who still fires the oven with wood. But in spite of the invidious fashion that is stealthily creeping in among certain layers of household on the continent for wrapped, ready-sliced loaves, bread is a food that is still taken seriously. There is no day of the week on which you cannot buy fresh bread in France. Daily you see customers choosing or rejecting certain loaves with the fastidious care usually applied to melons. They weigh in their hands and tap the bottom of a round *pain de campagne* (a loaf with a thick crust that lasts well) before taking the one they prefer. Some loaves are cut in half, weighed, and if a little underweight an extra nugget is added, so precisely is the business taken. Yet with all this attention over choosing a loaf, the way bread is treated once out of the shop appears offhand. Unwrapped, it's handled with perfunctory indifference. Tucked under an arm, clamped on to the carrier of a bicycle, or shoved down the back of a jacket if it's raining, bread is exposed to puddle splashes and lead exhaust fumes as it lies on the top of a shopping basket at just the right height to acquire an invisible coating of pollution.

Before the war it was common for farms and more substantial village houses to bake their own bread. Long-abandoned bread ovens can still be found in old farmhouses. The trouble is, what do you do with them? Ours in Shropshire, which we discovered behind the kitchen wall where we had intended to install the Aga, was so beautiful, so intact, that our cooker had to be fitted in elsewhere. The domed brick ceiling and the flat brick floor were perfect. The last baking could have been done the evening before and putting out my hand I half expected to feel warmth from the bricks and my palm to come away dusted with flour. Too deep to be a cupboard, the oven could only be used as a refuge for stoneware crocks and pitchers, and empty wine bottles too elegant to smash.

In France, which still has one of the highest consumptions of bread, the ovens were either integral to the house or else in separate buildings. I know of a family in the Creuse whose oven is apart from the house and where once a fortnight the farmer bakes enough loaves to last him and the rest of the extended family from one baking to the next. The little house becomes like a yeasty tea-cosy on a winter's day when the bitter wind cuts through the hills with perishing ferocity. Unlike our oven, where the fire was built underneath, this one has the fire built on the stone floor, where it has to reach an extremely high temperature before being used for baking. And the kneading, done in a long wooden trough, requires enormous staying power when mixing such large quantities; traditionally it was a man's job, which seems perverse when you consider that fetching water, an equally strenuous chore, is considered a woman's in most parts of the world. The oval woven baskets lined with linen in which the loaves are left to prove are identical to those shown in *Les Maîtres du Pain*, a film made in 1993 about a baker's family in the 1920s. For anyone interested in seeing an authentic country bakery and shop, they should watch this film. The details of rural life are touchingly depicted as well as drama, humour, and emotional fermentation all taking place among the rising dough and where bread-making methods appear to have changed little in seventy years. At least not at bakeries like Michel Pozzoli's in Lyon.

But alas nowadays you never see that practical and solid object, a *huche* (a wooden hutch, sometimes elaborately turned and decorated or more basically made with straight, unvarnished bars), hanging on a wall in which to keep the bread out of reach of children and dogs. Occasionally you can see one on a restaurant wall, empty, or find one covered in dust, the hinges broken, in a *brocante* shop. Only rarely, in some remote farmhouse, might you find one still in use.

All chefs feel passionately about bread. They talk about it, write about it, revere and praise it; bread is a symbolic and ritual ingredient in our lives as much as it is on the table. Water and fire, air, salt and grain are elemental; the taste, smell, look and texture are sensual attributes we respond to involuntarily. Shaun Hill, who until recently was the chef at Gidleigh Park in Devon, has now moved into another world and opened his own restaurant, the Merchant House, in Ludlow, Shropshire. He maintains that baking is as much at the heart of cookery as good stock. 'Palates are sharpest when stimulated by hunger; the smell of yeast, the crunch of crisp crust and the still warm taste of freshly-baked bread convince the punters that what is to follow will be good.' Such a relief. We've come a long way from Mrs Beeton's strictures that bread should never be eaten until it is at least a day old, for if we do we are coping with 'leathery poreless masses, which lie on the stomach like so many bullets'. Personally I'm crazy for those bullets.

Soft or low-gluten flour gives French bread its distinctive taste and texture and lowers the water content so that, according to Elizabeth David, you aren't condemned to carry home in your basket 'solidified water'. Pozzoli gets his flour from the near-by department of Ain, buying it from two or three different mills according to the kinds of bread he's making. In his shop, above the metal racks of bread is his own sign, *Les Mâitres du Pain*. Up-ended loaves are arranged in their different families or else piled in various shapes and tones of beige, brown or honey-colour in huge baskets along the counter. Their names roll off the tongue: *pain de ménage*, *pain aux germes* or *pain de seigle*; *campaillou* or *baguette*, *flûte* or *ficelle*.

The bread, made by the same method that has been used for generations, is baked in an oven fired by beech logs. 'I get a better crust from this wood,' Pozzoli told us. 'And what is more, a wood oven will stay warm longer than an electric one.' The fire is lit the night before when one of the men works till 1.30 am and one till 3.30. We watched Frederic, another of Pozzoli's employees, handle the *ficelles* tenderly as he lifted them out of a chest where they had been lying in shallow drawers, in floury troughs of pleated linen just as jewellers keep their long necklaces in velvet. Handled too roughly the loaves would die. He laid five at a time on wooden paddles which, when not in use, were balanced on a ledge above the oven. With a small curved blade he deftly slashed each loaf to give the bread its distinctive design, whether from single slashes, herring-bone patterns or hatched. The last load went in at noon. Between bakings he cleaned out the floor of the oven with a cloth on the end of a pole.

In Lyon there are two other *boulangeries cuit au bois*, but Michel Pozzoli's is the oldest, having for centuries been the bakery for a convent. Not only does he sell his bread in the shop, where his wife Miryam and sister-in-law Nathalie work, but he supplies it to specialist cheese shops who like to sell good bread alongside their produce. Altogether he makes about 1,000 loaves a day, as well as such things as quiches, savoury filled loaves and what sounds deliciously intriguing, a *feuilleté aux fruits de mer*. And there are shoals of cakes: morsels of lightness filled with praline, fragile shells containing honey and nuts dusted with cinnamon, *chapeaux de gendarmes* or *tuiles de chocolat aux amandes*; there are *galettes aux sucre, brioches pralinées*, colourful *tartes panachées* or boat-shaped tarts filled with apricots, raspberries or dark little dewy beads of bilberries under a transparent glaze.

But perhaps best of all, better than all the baking, which was driving us mad with its scents as well as its visual delectability, was the fact that Monsieur and Madam's son wanted to learn the trade. Unlike the farmers we spoke to in the Ardèche, whose children had no future on the land, this ten-year-old joined in our conversation, enthusiastically declaring his ambition to become a baker. How cheering. What a positive prediction to hear when so many *métiers* are putting up the shutters. We came away confident that the yellow van standing outside the shop, with *Votre Artisan du Quotidien* written on the side, will daily still be dodging the traffic of Lyon well into the next century.

I LIKE THE WAY THAT HERE AND THERE as you travel about the country, you can pick up little functional pamphlets that give you tips about eating. They aren't glossily produced with artwork or colour printing, but rather they're modest tracts acting like gastronomic pointers to head you in the right direction. For the bewildered they explain how to avoid suicide from eating Poison Pie fungi; what wine to drink with what; alternative ways with asparagus; or, as I picked up in Lyon, what bread to eat with what food. I may not follow the advice but I do appreciate the tip-off: 'Choose judicially,' they counsel. If you have a plate of *charcuterie*, try *pain de campagne* or wholemeal bread – both are stern stuff with a dense texture – but if you're having oysters then eat *pain de seigle*, rye bread, which goes well with any *crustacés* (shellfish). With sea or river fish then nothing but *pain aux germes* will do, but with meat and offal a rugged *pain paysan* tastes best, and rye bread with nuts or raisins in it is the one to eat with cheese. The list wanders on through a yeasty world with suggestions for suitable breads to accompany aperitifs, breakfasts, salads, game, white meat, *les crudités* and intestinal disorders. It seems there is a perfect bread for every occasion. Ah . . . what a blessed country.

Continuing on this subject, not bread but tracts, from the Ardèche I have a leaflet on table etiquette with advice on how to dress *une jolie table*; 'a harmony of colours is indispensable' from tablecloth, china and flowers; the flowers – a low bouquet – should be removed before your guests sit down and there must be forty centimetres between each diner. When confronted by a banana you may use your hands to peel one, but a fork is obligatory for eating, and be sure to wipe your mouth before drinking from your wine glass to avoid *des traces grasses*, greasy traces. Tips on mandatory dos and don'ts state that you may only *porter un os à sa bouche* if others are doing it first, and

when you do eat bones in your fingers, 'proceed with delicacy'; never dip and suck the same artichoke leaf twice; 'soldiers' dipped in a boiled egg are not *de rigueur*; never use a knife with salad; Americans, beware! never cut up all the meat before eating it, and to be truly *comme il faut* wait until the dessert course before placing ashtrays on the table, to discourage smokers from lighting up.

THERE'S A LOT TO BE SAID for going to restaurants out of season. It means that the new, purpose-built annexe, functional and characterless for summer tourists, is not yet in operation. Instead the guests can sit in the main part of the original building with its fireplace and cosy atmosphere where years of good meals have softened the corners, and the furniture, inherited from another era, is solid and immobile adding a sense of predictable stability which the patron has sensibly not yet replaced with schmaltzy tat. Sideboards and chafing dishes, candelabra and table linen are words long exiled from our vocabularies, but not always from dining-rooms. Or not from those restaurants where the owner has realized what is withering away before his eyes. The solid, functional objects may remain mostly as museum pieces along shelves, but in France in most places still, heavy cotton – often damask – napkins are more common than paper ones, even in quite humble establishments. (The same applies to bed linen. Travelling through France hotel visitors, more often than not, sleep between smooth-textured cotton sheets unadulterated by synthetics, even though drying them in winter must be far more lengthy.) The high-ceilinged, open-plan eating places trendy in London or Lyon have none of the reassuring comfort, the sense of being nannied, that comes with intimacy and maybe a certain shabby delapidation from fraying upholstery or corroding cruets.

We came to the Auberge des Chasseurs on Delphine's recommendation. Delphine, a young friend of Odile Masquelier, passed on addresses from her husband, a businessman who travels all over France and long ago sussed out reliable and economic *auberges* for the itinerant. This was one of his classier suggestions.

Auberge des Chasseurs
A STAR REFLECTED IN WATER

O N A SATURDAY MID-DAY in spring we were driving through the department of the Ain, still within the Lyon catchment area, only about thirty-odd kilometres away from the city. The song of frogs surrounds this part of France with its numerous lakes reflecting huge skies. The region of La Dombes between Lyon and Bourg-en-Bresse and between the rivers Ain and the Saône, has an understated charm. If you like the Norfolk Broads or the Fen country, you will respond to this watery landscape, which was flat and seemingly uninhabited, as we drove along lanes between sedgy pastures.

The village of Bouligneux is unremarkable, the juggernauts incessant, and the spasmodic barking of dogs a reminder of the restaurant's name. We liked the dining-room immediately. There was a serious feel to it. The two spoons and forks alongside one star in the

Michelin Guide meant we weren't expecting to find sumptuous lavishness in the décor. Shotguns and deer heads on the walls of the beamed room may be an indication of the menu in autumn but now, in spring, large vases of white and blue lilac filled the air with their soporific sweetness. And judging by the space between the white-clothed tables, laid with polished glasses and green and white plates,

there was ample room to bring up another table from which the waiter could serve. That's always a good sign. Microwaved food is served at speed with dire warnings to avoid touching the plates – a directive that never augurs well. But small tables ready to come alongside your own, as a tug-boat does to a liner, imply the waiter intends to spend time dishing up your meal before your eyes. It's a custom that's dying out. Later we were to meet chefs who admitted they now, more often than not, serve the food straight on to the plates in the kitchen rather than at table. How regrettable. There's a sense of luxury and cosseting in watching your food being dished up by someone else and the remainder left on the table under meat covers. The performance may not come up to that undertaken in the Second Empire, as described by Jean-Paul Aron in his fascinating book *The Art of Eating in France*, but even so it is one more passing skill to be regretted:

> He carves the meat in front of the diner in such a way that the latter can observe the dexterity and elegance with which this operation is carried out, then places the food on the plates so that the fragrance caresses his client's nostrils . . . his mouth waters.

A watering mouth! What a pleasurable offshoot to dining. It can be aroused at an outdoor picnic where lamb chops are grilling over wood; at a high-class restaurant in a city; at Chez Clotilde, with the *pot-au-feu* forever bubbling on the hob; or here in La Dombes where an aromatic trace of morels in butter came drifting round the tables. We'd had a long journey from the southern Ardèche that morning, driving through snow as we ascended towards Privas, so it needed little – a mere scent from the kitchen and the feel of our hands on the menu – to get our mouths watering.

Madame Dubreuil, the elegant wife of the chef, greeted us and showed us to our places. Two waitresses wearing conventional black dresses covered by white aprons added a sober note as they served at the tables. The pleasure of having time to linger over a menu while we dilly-dallied as to what to choose from an excellent list, should never be underestimated. In a way the meal begins then. Eating in the head is as potent as is gardening in the mind. And when the aperitifs arrived, accompanied by miniature terrines of salmon garnished with beads of tomatoes in olive oil and a delicately elusive flavour that none of us could name, we felt amiably pampered and in no hurry to do anything other than glide through the meal.

For our first courses Simon and I had asparagus in puff pastry, as friable as sandcastles, surrounded by a *langoustine* sauce which we spooned up, not wanting to miss a speck. David ordered prawns and avocado slices in an oil, lemon and dill dressing followed by carp and a classic cream sauce. (This freshwater fish is bred in La Dombes as well as in the mysterious region of the Sologne south of Orleans.) Simon's salmon steak was served with tomato and parsley noodles; I chose *grenouilles à la provençale*. We debated, but came to no conclusion, as to whether frogs are fish or meat. Simon, being a non-meat-eater, wasn't sure and, though tempted, left his decision to another day. Since then I see that Elizabeth David puts both snails and frogs into her fish section of *French Provincial Cooking*.

There was the choice of cheese one would expect to find in a restaurant of this class, fresh and varied with good Lyonnais Bleu de

Bresse and various goats' cheeses from the Mâcon area. *Crèmes brûlées* made in minute shallow, not deep, individual dishes so there was plenty of caramelized sugar were brought to table, before an overwhelming choice of desserts borne in on two trolleys that were more than we could cope with. Among them were a collection of fruits in syrup: small pears supporting caramelized oranges; apricots and syrupy strawberries; glossy cherries and *reine claudes*; figs, grapes, peaches all transfixed within glass bowls. The only other place where I've been faced by desserts on such a scale was at Le Prieuré set in gardens at Villeneuve-les-Avignon, where the food is unsurpassed and puddings way beyond the Plimsoll line of any sweet-toothed glutton. Confections of such creamy opulence, such well-endowed plumpness, of steamy dulcification and honeyed fruitfulness, not only send you tottering to bed but at breakfast, among the orange juice and cornflakes, they face you again. Any uneaten desserts are discreetly herded at one end of the breakfast buffet. Virgin bowls with the chocolate carapace intact and unsullied fluff piled peak beyond peak above syrupy meringues make us droop in shame, either as a reminder of last night's over-indulgence or else at our pathetic appetites next morning.

> For he on honey-dew has fed,
> And drunk the milk of Paradise

is small beer compared to living it up at Le Prieuré.

PAUL DUBREUIL (seemingly an auspicious Christian name for cooks) was helpful and articulate as we sat talking in a kind of small pantry between the kitchen and the dining-room. He was born in 1946 in the region outside Lyon. 'None of my family are in the business. I'm the only one.' He's been a cook since he was sixteen but before that his interests lay elsewhere. 'I was then thinking of either landscape designing – gardens – or reluctantly, cooking.' He certainly didn't want to choose cooking, 'because, you know, in the kitchen you work on Sundays!' And since he played football, that overrode any ambition to be a cook. When in 1959 at college he had a serious accident on the field and his mother banned him from the pitch, 'I took the decision. If I wasn't going to play football on Sundays any more – I would learn to be a chef.' After a three-year apprenticeship, he worked at various restaurants in Lyon, including the well-known Nandron on the quai Jean Moulin. 'There are chefs who cook *la cuisine moderne* – well, that's nearly everyone now – but there are other chefs who mix their products and style, and for me that's good.'

Even so his love of gardening has never been abandoned. He has a garden now and when there's time he goes outside to relax and enjoy another totally different area of creativity. Vegetables? 'No, no!' He was emphatic. 'A flower garden!' In May, when the *salle d'été* is working, he transplants geraniums, dahlias, petunias, begonias and *Impatiens* around the building to make a volatile entrance to the restaurant that would certainly catch the eye of any passing traveller dawdling through the village. While we talked we could smell the lilac between wafts of food being brought from the kitchen.

If he doesn't grow them, where then do the vegetables come from? 'I have a *marchand de légumes* – a greengrocer who delivers. You see in the region of Lyon we have a lot of vegetables: spinach, lettuces, carrots, turnips and so on – but little vegetables too – beans and peas, you know.' To the west, he told me, there's a micro-climate in the Monts Lyonnais, a region that gets only the north wind. It's there that

Simon Dorrell.

over the last twenty-five or thirty years, the farmers have transformed their farms to produce red fruit. 'It's well known for its abundance of *fruits rouges*. We've raspberries, redcurrants, blackberries, strawberries and, best of all, little wild strawberries.' And meat? Where does he get that from? 'From a local producer. He slaughters on the farm. He's both a farmer and a butcher at the same time.' Paul Dubreuil, who is sharp-eyed and earnest about what comes into his kitchen, knows the cattle from which the meat is produced: he's seen their pastures, watched their growth, and knows exactly how they are nurtured.

'For fish, frogs and *écrevisses* I work with a supplier – a wholesaler in Lyon.' Though the song of frogs surrounds us in this land of small lakes and meres, frogs for the restaurant are imported. Everyone is wheeling and dealing nowadays; even 'Greek' fetta cheese is made outside the country and then imported into Greece. How crazy can it get? Welsh lamb from South America? Dover sole from the Pacific and Dundee cake manufactured in Korea? Dubreuil's frogs come from Turkey, Egypt or Albania. Alive. But sadly not any longer from La Dombes.

Paul Dubreuil's use of local suppliers, whether a neighbouring farmer or a distributor in Lyon, underlines the slow collapse of markets. Even Rungis in Paris, that huge, sprawling bedlam full of hangars, is feeling the draught, but so are the native markets throughout France. More customers are using supermarkets, finding their produce fresh and cheap. There are exceptions: if you look for vegetables in the small chainstores like Sodi, Midi and even Casino, they are universally dreadful. They always look as if they have been in transit for far too long and have arrived already past their sell-by date. The best produce has always been found early, on open stalls. Now the vendors, in whatever size of market, are feeling an inevitable malaise; they are doomed, they've become one more endangered species which the pundits already prophesy by early next century will have gone for ever, overcome by the force of supermarket dominance.

Before we left the Auberge des Chasseurs I asked Dubreuil about his clients. 'Oh, they are local. They come from Lyon, from Villefranche and Mâcon. That is since we've been starred.' He achieved his first star in 1981 and, much to his credit and unlike so many others who shoot to brilliance and burn out after one or two years, he has kept it ever since. 'One star is very good for us.' And then he added with a certain wry wistfulness, 'You see, we're a little restaurant in this region, Bouligneux . . . ' He waved his hand, 'Over there is Lyon with three stars . . . I'm on my own here.'

RECIPES

SALADE LYONNAISE

THIS RECIPE USES EGGS POACHED **in red wine served warm on top of the salad; an alternative is to use *oeufs mollets*.**

SERVES 4
1 bottle Pinot Noir
8 eggs
salad leaves for 4 persons, such as a mixture of lambs' lettuce, oakleaf and curly endive
2 tbsp olive or walnut oil
1 tsp red wine vinegar
salt and pepper
75 g/3 oz smoked bacon, chopped
1 tbsp chopped fresh mixed herbs

BRING THE WINE TO THE BOIL in a shallow pan. Put in the eggs and poach for 3 minutes. Lift out the eggs with a slotted spoon.

Put the salad leaves into a bowl. Toss the leaves with most of the oil, the vinegar, salt and pepper and 1 tbsp of the wine cooking liquor.

Fry the bacon in a little oil and add to the salad leaves with the herbs. Place the eggs on top of the salad and serve.

POULET AVEC CRÈME ET MORILLES
CHICKEN WITH CREAM AND MORELS

POULARDE DEMI-DEUIL with truffles is a famous dish of Lyon. Here is an equally popular but less *recherché* alternative.

SERVES 4

2 tbsp seasoned flour
1.5–2 kg/3–4 lb chicken, divided into 8 – drumsticks, thighs and breast halves
75 g/3 oz/6 tbsp butter
1 small glass white wine
25 g/1 oz dried morels, soaked for 30 minutes in warm water
500 ml/18 fl oz/2¼ cups double (heavy) cream or crème fraîche
1 egg yolk
1 tsp lemon juice
salt and pepper

FLOUR THE CHICKEN PIECES and fry in the butter until browned. Pour in the wine and drained morels.

When the chicken is almost cooked, about 15 minutes, add the cream and braise for a further 15 minutes until tender.

Lift out the chicken pieces. Whisk in the egg yolk and lemon juice and check seasoning, adjusting if necessary. Pour the sauce over the chicken and serve with new potatoes or rice.

FRAISES ROMANOFF

PLACE STRAWBERRIES IN A BOWL and marinate in orange juice and Curaçao to taste. Stand the bowl in ice and cover the fruit with Chantilly cream (whipped cream and sugar).

Fondant au Chocolat

THIS IS THE RICHEST CHOCOLATE CONFECTION EVER, **meltingly squashy in the middle and covered by a brittle black carapace. I have tried the recipe several times since it was given to me. It is not complicated but best made 2-3 days in advance. Even chocolate fanatics who think they will have a second helping never can.**

SERVES 4–6

250 g/9 oz dark chocolate, grated

4 tbsp strong coffee

250 g/9 oz/1 cup plus 2 tbsp sugar

250 g/9 oz/1 cup plus 2 tbsp butter, diced

4 eggs, beaten

1 tbsp plain (all-purpose) flour

FOR THE ICING:

125 g/4½ oz chocolate

75 g/3 oz/6 tbsp butter

PLACE THE CHOCOLATE, coffee and sugar into a heatproof bowl. Melt slowly over a pan of warm water. Add the butter and stir until dissolved and thoroughly mixed. Add the eggs, then the flour. Put into a buttered 23 cm/9 in mould lined with nonstick baking paper (parchment).

Cook on top of the stove in a bain-marie (in a pan or shallow tin with sufficient water to come halfway up the sides of the mould) for 45 minutes.

Heat the oven to 150°C/300°F/Gas Mark 2. Transfer the dish to the oven and cook for 20 minutes. The top should look slightly undercooked when ready.

Melt the chocolate for the icing in a bain-marie. Add the butter. Stir until smooth. Turn out the icing and spread over the cake.

Chapter III

SI ON NE SAIT PAS,
ON FAIT
LE COULIS

Périgord

Chapter III
Périgord

Si On ne Sait pas, On Fait le Coulis

'SI ON NE SAIT PAS, ON FAIT LE COULIS.' What a revealing admission. The chef who produced this epigram had a wicked look as he threw out both his hands in a gesture of humorous confession. And the confession, that if one's stuck one can always make a *coulis*, is nowhere more relevant than in the Périgord and Quercy, in the department of the Lot and its neighbouring and equally large department, the Dordogne, overrun nowadays by *les rosbifs*.

Travellers in the past have invariably written about this area with either epicurean discrimination or with wolfish gluttony – but never, never with indifference. Such culinary eloquence will surely inspire us to travel hopefully, as well as arousing in us a rapacious appetite? Here are some of the comments gathered from pre-war travellers; from those who came to France in the 1950s freed from years of rationing; and others who more recently have trod the Périgordian lanes from village to village confident of finding their hedonistic nirvana among the restaurant tables of the province.

'There can be no doubt about it: Périgord is one of the regions in France where one dines best of all.'

'A friend motoring in France . . . was a little startled to find a number of persons seated at a table with their heads enclosed in pillow-cases . . . delighted sounds were emerging from these white hoods, and it was nothing more than a conference of gourmets trying out a new dish of truffles. The pillow-cases were to protect their palates from contamination by the outer world.'

'One feeds best in the countryside, where the food is grown (not imported) and cooked properly, for cooking is of primary (not secondary) importance in French schools.'

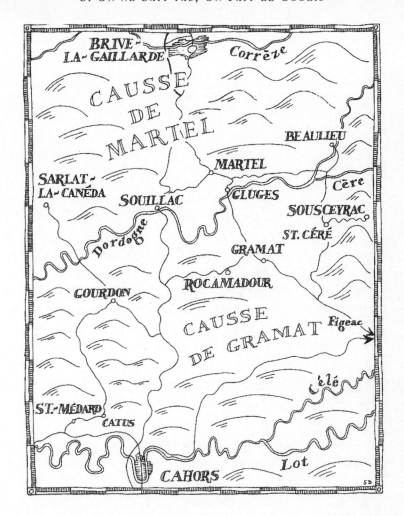

'... the country of black truffles and Roquefort cheese and walnut oil, of pigs and geese, and an immensely rich tradition of cookery ...'

'Beyond Limoges you are in the Dordogne, that magnificent land of strange, extinct volcanoes, limestone gorges and early churches, and, where appetites are concerned, *foie gras* and truffles.'

'You will find in this region no one thing that stands out supreme above others, but you will find everything to eat and drink that either *gourmand* or *gourmet* could possibly desire. You have come to heaven on earth!'

Promises! Promises! The *foie gras pâtés* of the Périgord were inlaid with black diamonds – the truffles of the countryside – blending their fragrance with the dense sensuality of the liver. Pike and eels, trout and crayfish came from the rivers; *confits*, walnut *pâtés* and walnut oil, and cooking based on goose fat, not butter, were commonplace. *Rillettes de porc*, truffled galantines, *ballotine de dinde*, *fonds*

d'artichauts au foie gras and *pâté* made from partridges filled with chicken liver and truffles, were standard fare on menus of the Périgord. Hare stuffed with pork, ham and spices; *enchaud périgourdin* – roast fillet of pork; sweetbreads flavoured with truffles; and for any back-sliding vegetarians – who do badly in this region – they could slum it, if they weren't averse to goose fat, on *pommes de terre sarladaise*, a potato and truffle pie. There were jams and fruit conserves, dried plums and *clafoutis* – a flan of black cherries. There was the golden ambrosia of Monbazillac wine and, if you could take one or the other, the cloying *crème* or *eau-de-noix*. And everywhere the dark muscular wine of Cahors spilled through the countryside.

We anticipated with upbeat spirits Cyril Connolly's Magic Circle stretching from Brive in the Corrèze south to Toulouse, and from Villeneuve in the Lot as far as Rodez in the Rouergue. His dream was to own 'A golden classical house, three storeys high, with *oeil de boeuf* attic windows and a view over water'. The houses are there yet, Mr

Connolly; the fair landscape and the slow rivers remain – but are the meals you used to eat? The stuff Simon, David and I had come to find? We hadn't yet read Frederic Raphael's requiem:

> The food of France, at every level and even in a traditionally delicious region like the Périgord, where we spend a good deal of our time, is losing its flavour, its honesty and its variety.

The land we were entering is a world of visual enticement: castles, manors, fortresses and turreted farmhouses with *pigeonniers;* rivers, cliffs and caves, and narrow pastures of bright green grass where cattle, the colour of Bath Oliver biscuits, graze. Fields of tobacco plants grow in sheltered valleys, and in autumn the barns are full of their drying leaves, the same colour as the many rusting farm implements rotting under a tangle of grass. Maize is stacked in golden walls within wire racks topped by a piece of corrugated iron. The crop is used for cattle fodder and the contentious *gavage* – force-feeding ducks and geese for *foie gras*; it's also used in *miques*, those regional dumplings which Michael and I used to try with unjustified optimism. The landscape was a dream of serenity with pigs contentedly grubbing among maize stumps; ducks and chickens wandering freely around farmsteads and flocks of geese waddling in the dappled light of walnut orchards or under stately poplar trees lining the river banks; blue smoke rose from chimneys and leggy dahlias were

turning brown. A woman in a dressing-gown sat sunning herself in a village street; an old man in a blue cotton jacket and slippers was buying meat from the travelling butcher while his dog leaped up at the counter scrounging for scraps, and the postman went into the café to sort his letters and gossip with the owner, who was preparing a dish of garlic, parsley and tomatoes, those kind of irregular-shaped tomatoes that keep their intrinsic flavour. The scene was timeless. The war memorial (touching testimonies of village families found throughout France) named nineteen who died in the First World War, six in the second and one in the *Guerre d'Algérie*. In wire pens three hounds were whimpering for their once-a-week Sunday reprieve when the master would take them to the killing fields.

Yet in spite of this pastoral sweetness, of all our journeys this was the most unfruitful. The most disappointing. We had no expectations of the Ardèche, which has never been extolled by articulate travellers for its cuisine, but the Périgord – where the cooking 'is fit for kings'? That had been our Eldorado.

Also we were ignorant. We didn't know that many places have their *fermeture annuelle* in October. Unable to keep going any longer – until the more usual months of January or February, say – exhausted proprietors sag with fatigue from months of tourism. All they want to do is escape; to batten down the hatches the moment the last foreign number-plate disappears round the corner. Who can blame them? But for us, coming in the perfection of autumn, it was a body blow. The roads were empty, certainly, but so too were the restaurants. Even good and remembered *charcuteries* may be closed for their annual holiday at this time of year.

Perhaps the *coup de grâce* was finally struck for us when, after reading 'most people in the Dordogne will wish to savour its culinary delights in the countless excellent and cheap restaurants of the Périgord', we lunched at a humble *auberge* along the Dordogne river on soup from a packet, manufactured terrine and uniform rabbit cubes nestling in a glutinous gunge. Another day we fled from a life-sized figure of a waitress with nylon hair wearing a thigh-high naughty-maid's uniform, a corsage of plastic flowers, high heels and a frilly apron to which the menu was pinned. Were we too faint-hearted? Perhaps; for we rejected, too, a one-star restaurant framed by a hedge the blue of metallic car-finish, where the turquoise swimming pool sucked colour from the surroundings and a waiter with a hoover sucked up fallen leaves. The restaurant was empty.

By now we were getting desperate. Where could we eat? Wherever we turned we seemed to be faced with one more example of Frederic Raphael's verdict or Paul Bocuse's pithy condemnation: '*Le Périgord, de beaux produits, oui, mais de l'année dernière.*' Ah those *années dernières*. Only three years ago, further south on another river, away from this culinary disaster area, we had the opposite experience. It was early afternoon when we stopped at a restaurant in a village on the Célé, a lovely river – a mere vein, compared to the great arteries that cut through western France – where at places tawny cliffs rise clear out of the water. There were diners on the terrace; a party of middle-aged French revellers eating so well there wasn't a scrap of food left. The four of us must have looked so downcast that Madame took pity, she said that if we didn't mind eating what they themselves ate, and if we didn't mind sitting in the kitchen, she would feed us with pleasure.

On the table she put down a large bowl of hare terrine, the kind that is meant to last the week by merely covering the uneaten section with an eiderdown of lard. The spices, pistachio nuts, shallots, herbs and brandy made it one of the best terrines we'd eaten. We drank so much Cahors wine that I've forgotten what followed after. All I remember is that the occasion was memorable for being unexpected and hospitable and nourishing.

But now, despondent with little hope of finding Freda White's 'gastronomical paradise', we risked returning to a place where Michael and I had eaten ten years ago. *Le Gindreau.* Were we mad to return? The chances were, Yes. But the chances of finding anywhere good were slim when around the corner the word 'Snack' assaulted us; we felt we had little to lose. The paucity of good meals in a land so obviously oozing with fecundity was increasingly disheartening.

The restaurant is on the outskirts – if you can have outskirts to a hamlet of fewer than 200 people – of St Médard, overlooking a narrow valley where the stream Vert twists its way down to the Lot. In the glossy light of autumn, shadows appeared blue among groves of vines and maize interspersed by patches of meadow grass where a few walnut trees idled through the landscape. The setting was idyllic, peaceful and so unfrequented that the only vehicle was a tractor loaded with giant cotton-reels of hay.

Le Gindreau
'I Shall Teach My Children about Good Food'

G ERANIUMS WERE FLOWERING in pots along the balustrade, and on the terrace heavy wooden tubs of hibiscus and lemon trees gave the place a southern feel. The tubs had wheels under them; any day frost was expected and they'd be wheeled away and the chestnut trees shading the tables would cast their leaves overnight. My spirits rose. From the outside the place hadn't changed. But what of the restaurant?

Inside a transformation had taken place. The room was one of the prettiest we'd eaten in. Yellow walls and lampshades produced a warm light which was accentuated by vases of chrome sternbergias on each table in a high-ceilinged room with an elegant fireplace. The auspices were promising; we felt buoyant enough to try *kir* made with walnut liqueur – it was over-sweet – which came with miniature porcelain dishes of quails' eggs in sauce. They were the *mise en bouche*, a fashion that has taken over everywhere and must send the chef to sleep each night mentally fiddling with little bits of food.

The appearance, smell, texture and taste of the dishes we chose (from a menu with suggestions for a glass of the appropriate wine to drink with each course) were superb: a fillet of salmon in a cloud of tarragon sauce; broad beans, peas and lentils served with meat taken from pigs' trotters, enveloped in cabbage leaves and covered with crispy breadcrumbs; mushrooms in a garlicky *velouté* sauce, smooth, creamy and based on veal stock, served with tiny rounds of toast (I was offered a second helping). We ate squid filled with mussels and basmati rice; pink slices of roast *noix d'agneau*; *confit de canard* lying among white haricot beans and the unctuously rich ingredients that make up a cassoulet. The self-important *sommelier* was continually pitching round the tables like a figure of Peter Ustinov at sea. We drank a Cahors wine, Domaine Grauzile 1988, as substantial as port and not too fruity.

The delicious cylindrical cheese from the Auvergne, Fourme d'Ambert and local *brebis de Catus* were served with hot *pain de raisin*. But the breathtaking surprise were the coral-coloured dollops of quince purée accompanying the cheese. What a brilliant union: better by far than the trend in England of serving grapes on the same dish as the cheese. The combination of tastes, the invigorating sharpness, were perfect. My quince tree at home never has enough sun to turn the fruit large and yellow, yet quinces are one of the world's supreme fruits; when they're cooking their invasive scent envelops the house in a powerful astringency.

We ended the meal with cinnamon and apple purée with walnut ice cream; *crème caramel*; and a coffee mousse (room temperature, not straight from a freezer cabinet) with *chocolat fondant*. Afterwards we had coffee and homemade *petits fours* on the terrace under the trees where Alexis Pelissou, the chef, joined us.

Pelissou and his wife, Martine, after working in Toulouse and having knocked about a bit – 'roulé un peu' – have made a lot of

changes since they came to St Médard in 1974. But almost uniquely among restaurant conversions they haven't taken apart the very reason for the building's distinction any more than they have eroded the standard of cooking. The building's present *soigné* elegance may conceal its origins as a schoolhouse built in 1903, but the tall school windows, the symmetry of design, the *oeil de boeuf* in the pitched roof and the decorative finials are all unscathed.

Pelissou is fiercely positive about the way cooking is going. 'I don't think we should give up! The rising generation is receptive to good cuisine.' He spoke with passion. 'I watch my children. I intend to teach them! When one serves them something good – well – they appreciate it.' He laughed with the confidence of someone who knew he was in control and succeeding. He wasn't going to droop under the weight of proliferating pizzas. And unlike some cooks and market vendors who lament the changing fads, he was adamant, 'It's not true to say that the younger generation don't know how to eat. It's simple! We must just offer them good things! Then they, in their turn, will make them – and so the dishes will be perpetuated.'

In spring a plate of *morilles* and truffles is his idea of noble eating. 'I like to work with nature . . . ' He looked around, waved his arms and spoke ardently about the good things to be had. 'There's *le pain à l'ancien*, and in the Lot there's the wine – le Cahors. There are people who take their wine-making very, very seriously – well – I think – once one has wine and bread – oh, yes – and the cheese – one can't go wrong.' His enthusiasm rippled off in waves of sparkling affirmation. It was hard not to be infected by it, especially having first been here when he was a young man and the cooking even then had been so memorable we'd never forgotten it.

In reply to my question about the differences, if any, between the neighbouring *départements*, he said, 'I think in the Lot one finds *l'influence occitale*, then there's cooking that comes from the Périgord, but also there's *une poussée* from the Cantal. Somewhere all these cuisines meet. In addition to which, of course, are the high-class gastronomic products – the truffles, the *foie gras*, etc.' The Cantal? The cheese, you mean? 'Yes, but it's more on the *charcuterie* side I'm speaking about.' And to the south, in the Gers, Aveyron and the Haute-Garonne? 'Well, the Gers is a region for poultry. Doctors would confirm that between the Gers and the Aveyron the difference is that in the Gers the people feel well, they eat poultry – and on the other side they feel well because they don't eat poultry, they eat *charcuterie* and *foie gras*! So there you have two *départements* quite distinct.' Pelissou was enjoying himself. 'As for us in the Lot, we have the best of both worlds: *le canard gras*, the fatty duck which gives us our winter cooking – our *cuisine hivernale* – because it's conserved and then we have the *cèpes* that feature so much in our cuisine.' But the meat, you haven't spoken of it? 'The meat is lamb. We call the local sheep *les moutons à lunettes* because of the black circles round their eyes. They used to predominate on the Causses de Gramat, but shepherding is dying out.' Yet he didn't sound downcast, or yearning for the past; he seemed to be confident and happy. 'We have a good balance, if you like, between the lamb, the duck, the geese and the *foie gras*. It's all right!' And if you eat out? 'Well, we have so many *restaurateur* friends that it's the *casse-tête chinois* to choose. But we don't do it often because when we do meet up with friends – well – *on*

mange, on se régale, puis après . . . ' His sentence tailed off in a shrug
– after eating, enjoyment, and then . . .

When we told him that we were going to Alsace in November he
was emphatic. 'I shall tell you where to eat!' He wrote down the
address of a restaurant and then told us that on no account should we
miss going to a *winstub* where the owners were particularly good
friends of theirs. At the time I little knew how grateful I should feel
towards Alexis Pelissou. We were fairly sanguine by now; so many
recommendations had been fallacious, not intentionally, but because
the place had declined into a microwave joint, or it was empty.

THERE'S A TENDENCY when writing about France to go on about
markets. Travelling as we did in such diverse regions, we
gravitated compulsively in their direction. Without volition, as though
blindfolded, we walked towards them, arms outstretched, to feel and
smell new sensations; to uncover alien tastes and ingredients,
prepared to be intrigued, even inspired. But it doesn't always work
like that. First you may have to wade through car tyres in unappealing
piles and rivers of hideous clothing; stalls of synthetic black cycle
jackets, polyester pullovers and children's garments of such ugliness
they'd wither the soul of any child. Yet in between there are gems; not
necessarily to buy, but to feel and ponder over, such as old men's vests
– garments reaching to the knees to droop over equally floppy long-
johns; platoons of clasp knives fitting into the palm like a friend's
handshake; slippers so cosy you almost fall asleep as you yawn over
the display; and always, somewhere, stout cotton drying-up cloths,
smaller than ours, but made for wrapping around a piece of bread,
saucisson and cheese to be taken into the field or stuffed into the
pocket of a shepherd's greatcoat. Then, if you've manoeuvred past
this vast Sargasso Sea of inedibles, you may move into the market
proper. The bit we've come to see. And if it happens to be the Saturday
market in Sarlat you have a treat ahead; not for the produce only, but
for the medieval, Renaissance and seventeenth-century setting.

Those narrow lanes running between the tall houses of apothe-
caries, scholars and merchants must surely be one of the finest sites

anywhere for a market. Scattered around the cathedral and in the network of alleys were stalls luminous, on a grey day, with colour from the fruit and vegetables. One woman had a modest display of orange pumpkins, brown eggs, a bucket of Michaelmas daisies and a bunch of Chinese lanterns lying at her feet. Once in Sarlat when we'd come to buy a kettle – before we discovered they're non-existent in France – we ended up by talking food with the shopkeeper who, waxing lyrical over walnuts, gave us the recipe for walnut mousse which his wife makes from *bleu de Quercy* cheese mixed with butter and folded into whipped *crème fraîche*. Chopped nuts are added last. 'It's scrumptuous!'

Sarlat is the town of salamanders. The glossy black and yellow Fire Salamanders are found across the whole of central and southern Europe. Numerous relics of the reptile were discovered among the watery ground on which Sarlat was built, and images of the beast symbolize the town for having withstood fire and for enduring the centuries. The legend grew from their habit of hibernating in logs; when thrown on the fire the heat drew the creatures out and they appeared among the flames, invulnerable. Surely here, of all places, I would find a *quincaillerie* selling salamanders? But life isn't that simple: there wasn't an ironmonger in the rue de la Salamandre. We did go to one in the rue de la République – La Traverse – a road brutally slicing through the town like a scar from an abdominal operation. The ironmongery was good; David found a black-handled, pointed kitchen knife he'd been hankering after for some time. When he went to pay we were delayed somewhat by the soft-hearted shopkeeper who was reluctant to push aside the dangling tail of his cat, settled on top of the cash register, which was concealing the numbers.

I N MY NOTEBOOK for 12 April 1977 I record how, after leaving St Céré, we climbed up a winding road through leafless woods. The pall of winter lay over everything. The road was empty; nothing passed us as we made our way to the restaurant Au Déjeuner de Sousceyrac in an undistinguished village on the edge of nowhere. Entering a darkly-beamed dining-room, warm from a log fire and redolent with cooking, we were welcomed by Madame Espinadel. What followed was a meal of unexpected and delectable perfection starting the best way ever, with an *omelette aux truffes*. The sliced truffles had been left in a bowl of beaten eggs to allow their mysterious smell to percolate (there is supposed to be an acknowledged symbiosis between eggs

and truffles) before the mixture was turned into a pan of barely-sizzling butter and the eggs were cooked until they were about to solidify but hadn't quite. It was the first time we'd eaten truffles; the delicacy and scent were so indescribable we were left temporarily speechless from an experience that haunts me still. It was the moment to *ronron*, that onomatopoeic word for purr, which is the way my grand-daughter Cassandra, regardless of where we are, shows gutsy approval whenever she's eating something she particularly likes. On that occasion our *ronrons* would have lapped the room with appreciative murmurings.

We never ate truffles again. However the memory of the occasion is branded on my culinary skin even if I can no longer conjure up the taste any more than I can recall the scent. After the omelette a solitary endive salad preceded *bouchées* filled with *cèpes* and sweetbreads in *sauce à la crème*, with a separate dish of braised salsify. My notes don't go further. My memory has evaporated.

The starred restaurant was at that time run by the Espinadel family. Madame was front-of-house, her husband was the chef and their son, Pierre, helped around the place. We used to stay the night in the austere bedrooms with old-fashioned sagging beds, grand *armoires* –

they have now become chic and expensive but at that time could be bought for little – dicey plumbing, intermittent heating and the kind of vulgar wallpaper I love: blowsy flowers so hideously outrageous they forced me to close my book and eyes as quickly as possible. We loved the place. I can't remember how many times we made the long journey across the bleak uplands from the Cantal for the sake of eating dinner there. The Cantal was country we frequented; not for its food – Sousceyrac was the first place for good eating coming from an easterly direction before descending to the flesh-pots of the Lot – but for the valleys and isolation of the Cantal, the marginal farming, and the sound of running water and distant cow bells. The cattle of the Cantal are superb. They have eyelashes an actress would kill for, decorative horns, and are russet brown, matching the bracken on the upland slopes of the Cirque de Falgoux and the Vallée de Medailles. We knew every thread of a road leading off the valley of the Maronne; one June we were turned back from an eastwards journey across the *massif central* by snow on the Puy Mary another time, heading north, by snow on the gaunt uplands of the Millevaches Plateau.

Pierre, the son, was young and talkative in those days, keen to ask us where in London he could go to improve his English as he wanted to become a chef. I don't imagine we were much help – we didn't live in London – but with Pierre's lively gusto he would land on his feet wherever he chose. How cruel. He died too young, in 1987, after a long illness.

Au Déjeuner de Sousceyrac
On the Edge of Nowhere

'A SIMPLE SMALL SALAD, some lentils, a little sausage – all cooked very well – that would be good! But it's not done any more. Everything is bought in packets – frozen!' Two decades after our truffle feast, this bleak judgement was made by the present *patron-chef*, Richard Piganiol, in the foyer of his hotel after we'd eaten a remarkably good meal.

We started with the prescribed *amuse-bouche*. It was unusual: slices of spicy *boudin noir*, no bigger than a fifty-pence coin, served on apple slithers. This should be easy to make at home, but I know I'll never do it, for, unless you make them yourself, our bought black puddings are more solid and less spicy than the French breed. While we ate chicken breast stuffed with liver; monkfish and salmon; slices

of duck in a dark Cahors sauce accompanied by individual *gratins dauphinois* turned out like castle puddings, we watched somewhat enviously a couple at the neighbouring table (who never spoke to each other throughout the meal) having as a first course fish of some sort under a pastry lid in the classic white soup bowls with ears. The dome of golden pastry, as they broke in and let the steam out, smelled irresistibly appetizing. For his dessert Simon chose well, perhaps his artist's eye had already anticipated the roasted figs lying in their blue-black plum sauce beside an amber peach sorbet.

Richard Piganiol was born in Sousceyrac, a village of about a thousand inhabitants, and had gone to school there. 'I was very undisciplined!' It wasn't difficult to imagine. He still had a roguish vigour about him, unlike some of his more solemn *confrères* in the business. 'When I was at school – well – I didn't know a thing about cooking. Of course I liked cooking – and all that. And then once I was at the *lycée*, I needed to earn pocket money. I came here – I worked in the cellar sorting out bottles and all that. *Alors*, one day, Pierre asked me – because one of the staff was sick – to lend a hand peeling vegetables – tomatoes, and all that. And that's how I began. I enjoyed it!' The first thing he remembers learning to cook was a trout.

Later, when Piganiol was living in Paris and undergoing his apprenticeship in a hotel, he never lost touch with Pierre; when Au Déjeuner began to go downhill through Pierre's illness, and lost its star, Piganiol returned to Sousceyrac. It was the beginning of a new life he has never once regretted.

The hotel and restaurant were in a bad way owing to the tragedy in the Espinadel family. With the vigour of youth, Richard and his Parisian wife Laurence, who is beautiful and vivacious, have revived Au Déjeuner by re-decorating and upgrading the facilities without going over the top. New ceiling, uplighting and an overall burnishing of the dark room and its old-fashioned furniture have changed the restaurant's persona. From the outside it looks much the same, unostentatious and a place for serious eating. 'When I first returned,' said Piganiol, 'I continued with cooking much as we had done in Paris – *le confit, les magrets* and a great deal of fish. But now – we're going back to more traditional cooking. Regional cooking.' In summer there are tourists; plenty of English, of course, but Belgians, too, who have 'very good stomachs!' Laurence said with obvious pleasure. During the other seasons they have to rely on French clients who come from near-by St Céré or as far away as Clermont-Ferrand. Retrieving the one-star Michelin rating two years ago has meant everything to them. 'Without the star,' Laurence said, 'we'd do badly. Having a star makes people come from further around. They look in the *Michelin*, see the star and will come forty or fifty kilometres for a meal.'

The menu varies a lot, depending on resources and the season. At present there's game: '*Gibier* and all that. Hare, venison, wild boar.' (Oddly it was the first place in this region where we had seen chicken or pork on the menu.) But whenever they themselves go out to eat they look for little bistros, not *les grandes tables* but for '*une petite chose familiale*'. When I lamented the loss of these little bistros and

family-run places, he agreed. 'Now *il n'y a plus.*' And Laurence added, 'The Dordogne is a tourist trap. People just want to make money.' She was derisive, 'They aren't professionals – *c'est tout*!'

And other chefs. Whom do they admire? 'There is one who does things I really like! said Piganiol. 'He's Pacaud at L'Amroisie in Paris. His cooking is modern, but at the same time it's traditional.' He paused, put his head on one side, and added, 'But then there are different ways in the kitchen! That is to say when there are four of you in the kitchen one can do good things. And if you are twelve, you can do very good things – and when you are twenty, you can do fine things, but differently again. What is interesting is the product – the taste – the smell – and the look.' He laughed, 'But with some – it's only *le grand spectacle*!' Yes. And not only in France; England has some fairly histrionic performers. 'We want to make different marriages in the cuisine,' Richard went on, 'but we don't invent.'

The winter is long at their altitude of 559 metres; Laurence's home town is the other side of an immense and windswept landmass. I asked her about the winter, when the restaurant is shut and when the area closes in on itself. 'So far I haven't missed my life in Paris!' She is not homesick, she said, but she does sometimes get depressed. I hope they keep their star. 'Ah, we just cross our fingers!' And she smiled.

IN THE TOWN OF GOURDON near where David, Simon and I were staying, Michael and I would sometimes buy our wine from a cavern full of barrels. The old man who kept it let us sit and taste this or that wine, before filling up our empties while he kept up a running account of the year's grape harvest. In the same town, until a few years ago, Madame Cassagne at La Maison du Fromages used to sell *vins fins* and wine *en gros*. With infinite concern she'd suggest which wine to drink with which cheese, or which cheese to go with which wine, according to the way one attacked it. And this in a town with fewer than 5,000 inhabitants. Such pleasures are the breath of life to shopping in France.

I was disappointed to find that the *charcutier-traiteur* – where Madame Carré makes the best walnut *pâté* in the world, and *confit* from goose, spices and herbs, embalmed in its own fat so that it keeps for a year – was shut for its annual holiday. Consequently the other *charcuterie* was doing brisk business. David and I were lured in by seeing its blackboard with the day's ready-cooked *endive au jambon, émincé de dinde, paupiettes de veau* and *langue de boeuf sauce tomate*. All dishes that had been made on the premises. How I wish we had this

tradition in Britain. Often in France we used to buy ready-made *chou farci* or on Fridays the quite delicious, but such a bore to make, *brandade de morue*. (A rich amalgam of salt cod, garlic, milk and olive oil.) We'd take the prepared dish back to the house where we were staying, and warm it for our supper. Simple, inexpensive and so civilized.

On this occasion David and I were late arriving at the *charcuterie*. The first bowl of *rillettes d'oie* was already empty. The new one, uncut, was covered with a snowy blanket of fat which Madame rolled back to reveal the mushroom-coloured mixture beneath. She told us she made it from goose, shredding the meat by hand with two forks, with some of its fat plus seasoning but nothing else. It was fibrous, succulent and very rich. We ate it with chunks of bread, red wine and a salad dressed – how could we do otherwise? – with walnut oil. It's not often, in restaurants, that a stout earthenware pot of *rillettes*, the kind Clotilde used to make as a matter of course, is put on the table for you to serve yourself, but there are compensations for these changes: thrushes cooked with juniper are now no longer on menus.

'A few miles away lies Souillac, a little town which, I was about to write, has already the taste of the south in it, but, in fact, what it is unavoidable to taste, in Souillac, are the truffles. It is famous for them.

This is one of the towns in France where the food is so good that it interferes, seriously, with sight-seeing.' Sacheverell Sitwell wrote this in 1953. In 1994 in the École Hôtelière Quercy-Perigord in Souillac, where you can eat what the students cook, their menu started off with Cocktail Florida. For Sitwell today, sight-seeing would obviously have no rival.

If you're in this region in October there is no avoiding walnuts. You may even be lucky enough to eat a heap of halved walnuts, fresh, moist and slightly bitter, offered as a first course on an imaginative menu. Briefly soaked in white wine vinegar with green peppercorns and tarragon, they are dressed with olive oil, seasoning and *verjus*. Whereas butter is used in the north, and olive oil around the Mediterranean, in the west, from the Limousin to the Pyrénées and through the Charentes, Périgord and Quercy, walnut oil is the basic ingredient. And its production is on the increase. Youthful orchards are flourishing. Wherever we went we saw nuts being shaken from trees (whose straight trunks and oval leaves looked like those a child draws) by small groups of people, with none of the intensity of the grape harvest that has to be done at the crucial moment. Walnut gathering appeared more like olive harvesting when a violent storm would bring out the women and children to gather the fallen fruit. Nuts lay scattered across the narrow country roads, tempting a passer by to pick them up. But those lying on the verge do belong to someone and only those in the road can be legitimately gleaned. Sturdy trugs for the harvest are sold in the market, arranged in families so that there's a size to suit everyone; once home the nuts are left drying in shallow wooden boxes outside farmhouses.

Near the medieval town of Martel we visited a walnut mill. In the nineteenth century every community had its press, but after the Second World War they were abandoned. Now, in the last twenty years, there's been a revival in walnut-oil production and a number of mills, whether worked by electricity or water, are being restored. Geared for tourists, the dark pieces of ancient equipment in the mill we visited were carefully roped off from the public; the cobbled floor was glossy from oil and the gloomy room smelt deliciously biscuity. In the past there used to be convivial *soirées dénoisillage* when, in winter, the family and neighbours gathered together for nut-breaking evenings, using small wooden hammers to extract the kernels.

The pressing took place in three stages: first the nuts were crushed with enormous stone wheels that were worked by mules or horses; next the paste was heated over a fire in a copper or enamel pan, which had to be stirred continually with a long-handled paddle until the crucial moment when the pan was withdrawn. The millers trusted their noses as to when to do this. The longer it cooked, the stronger the taste. Lastly came the pressing, when the hot paste was squeezed in the *pressoir*. As in the land of olives, where village mills have largely been abandoned, farmers now take their crops to be pressed at a central mill, both mechanical and labour-saving.

APART FROM A FEW EXCEPTIONS we knew by now that the 'perfumed soul' of the Périgord was eluding us. We'd read the tales. We'd been lulled into gastronomic fantasies. And in what had seemed wildly extravagant claims for the richness of the region, we'd lingered in disbelief over travellers' accounts: 'Fine, gradiloquent superlatives may be applied without qualm to the genius of Périgourdine cooks.'

Without qualm? Well, if you say so. Our qualms, by now, had a high profile after a recent meal of trout in chunks and wine from glasses tasting of detergent.

Where does one eat? I'd come to the conclusion that all the recommendations, or most of them, which had been given to me through French and English connections were red-herrings: that is, people I had contacted for advice hadn't wanted to appear churlish, but nor did they want to risk some treasured bistro appearing in print. Anyone who knew of a good restaurant wisely kept it to themselves. They didn't want culinary vandalism to overwhelm one of their sequestered *auberges*; fearful of the place being Peter Mayle'd, they thrust lists of compromises into our hands so that we wasted hours peering at menus and through curtained dining-rooms before wandering disconsolately through terrain gone stale on pizzas. I sympathize. For years friends of ours were sworn to silence over a village we used to take them to high in the Pindus mountains.

However, one friend of a friend was memorable. She lives in a beautiful house in the heart of Martel and, without hesitation, she advised us to try Les Falaises at Gluges. The village is on the Dordogne and not far from the ominously horrible Rocamadour, clamped to the cliff face, whose bad vibes rise from the chasm like a spiritual defoliant. On the way to Gluges we passed a car park where clients were being transported by miniature railway to a near-by restaurant, with such gimmicky success that the place was packed to the gunwales with French diners. In contrast Les Falaises was almost empty; but then it had no railway, nor did it have white globular lamps like oversized footballs along a parapet overlooking the calm tranquillity of a willowy tributary. Les Falaises, tucked comfortably under cliffs, has creeper-clad walls and a terrace for fine-weather eating.

Restaurant Les Falaises
'I LEARNT FROM MY GRANDMOTHER'

THE CONFIT D'OIE POUR DEUX PERSONNES instantly restored our faith: in the lady from Martel, in the food of the Périgord, and even in the euphoric pronouncements of past travellers. We were redis-covering the joy of one of the world's greatest pleasures by eating a recipe of venerable grandeur. And because we'd come to expect indifference, David and I devoured our meal with intemperate gratification through savoury joints tenderly swathed in sauce. I could have fallen off my chair in astonishment. When you arrive mentally dyspeptic, the appetite can quicken in an instant.

Good *confit* can't be prepared beforehand. 'The sauce must be done at the last minute. Nothing can be done in advance if it's to taste just right,' chef Jean-Michel Dassiou declared. To keep us going his wife brought us fresh *cabécou* coated with chopped walnuts served on salad with a walnut oil and lime dressing. The pieces of *confit* have first to be removed from their protective nests of fat, cleaned scrupulously of all the *graisse*, before being used in whatever way the chef has chosen. It must also come to the table warm, not hot.

Dassiou's *confit* was meltingly succulent, done in a *bouillon* and butter sauce with *cèpes* imbued with garlic and parsley, followed by the astringent taste of a fresh green salad: pure and unadorned except for a dressing.

Dassiou had been born in the house. 'My grandparents lived here. Then my parents, and now me. I'm the third generation.' He worked

in Toulouse, then in Paris at various restaurants including the classy Hôtel Bristol, before he and his wife took over Les Falaises, where they've been for the last eleven years. His grandparents, from whom Dassiou learnt so much, went in for very traditional regional cooking.

Although he thinks *nouvelle cuisine* is deadly, he does acknowledge that the fashion did demand the best of fresh produce, 'which can't be a bad thing!' Perhaps this is its most worthwhile legacy because as Dassiou remarked, 'It's increasingly difficult to find good restaurants in France where the ingredients are fresh. Take Rocamadour, for instance, it's horrible! Every two metres and there are hamburgers and fast-food bars – it's always potatoes or something frozen.' He's a great vegetable disciple. 'Lots of vegetables – five or six – whether raw, cooked, hot or cold. There's no doubt vegetables are a lot of work – but it's better.' He prefers to cook simple things, he says, such as chicken in *verjus* or grilled lamb, and in the winter, pork. (His recipe for *poulet sauté au verjus* is given at the end of the chapter.)

'We kill the pigs in winter and it's then that we eat *la tête pressée.*' A process that few would tackle with a pig's head today, I imagine, even though in *Charcuterie and French Pork Cookery*, Jane Grigson leads you through the procedure step by step. It used to be made with truffles, but can you imagine anyone who'd got truffles as far as their kitchen pausing long enough to go through such an elaborate performance with the head of a pig? I think Dassiou said he made his *tête pressée* with pistachio nuts. He's also very particular about what his pig is fed. 'If we had pork on the menu throughout the year, we wouldn't have a well-raised, well-nourished animal,' he explained. He keeps everything left over from the restaurant for his pigs. '*Chantilly* cream, *gâteaux* – everything! My friend looks after them for me and they are fed on the best from Les Falaises!' In that way he feels satisfied knowing exactly what sort of pork will end up on the table. 'But it's comic,' he exclaimed, 'because for three months when the restaurant's closed and we haven't enough for the pigs, they refuse to eat for several days. The creatures sulk! Even though my friend feeds them on potatoes and pumpkins – and other good things – they aren't interested.' Presumably in spring, when you open up again, everything changes? '*Voilà!*'

On the *spécialités régionales* menu for last August which Dassiou showed me, four out of ten dishes were for duck, two for goose and the others either for chicken, omelettes or ham. No fish? 'We are landlocked,' he told me, 'and La Rochelle is distant.' Tourism and pollution have had a devastating effect on streams and rivers that used to 'abound with trout, pike, perch and other freshwater fish, including the *écrevisses* . . .'. There aren't even minnows to be caught and treated like whitebait. 'But,' he cheered up, 'for the moment we have St Jacques from the Channel! That's for today! It's a little menu that I made *comme ça, pour aujourd'hui.* You see, it all depends on the produce that I can get hold of.'

Before we left he promised to send me a recipe, his grandmother's. 'Then I'll know that when I'm an old, old man my grandmother's recipe is still living!'

Recipes

Millefeuille de Pommes de Terre et Foie Gras
Potato and Foie Gras Millefeuille

RICHARD PIGANIOL uses a potato available in France called Roseval for this dish. Here Pink Fir Apples are a possible substitute, as a friend discovered when trying out this recipe. However, it is essential to use small potatoes that will slice into small, neat discs.

Serves 4
1 kg/2¼ lb potatoes, peeled
salt and pepper
1 tbsp oil
butter for cooking
250 ml/8 fl oz/1 cup port
250 ml/8 fl oz/1 cup red wine
500 ml/18 fl oz/2¼ cups veal stock
2 medium leeks, cleaned
500 g/18 oz raw foie gras

HEAT THE OVEN to 200°C/400°F/Gas Mark 6. Cut the potatoes in thin rounds. Lay them in a 'rose window' circle in the bottom of eight 7 cm/2¾ in diameter moulds. Sprinkle with salt, pepper and a little oil, and add a knob of butter to each. Place on a baking sheet and cook for about 20 minutes until tender.

Place the port, red wine and stock in a saucepan and simmer until well reduced to a sauce. Finely mince the leeks, blanch in a pan of boiling water for 2 minutes then sweat in a little butter for 5 minutes. Cut the foie gras into 8 slices (allowing 2 slices per person) and gently cook in butter for a few minutes.

Arrange the leeks on the base of four heated serving plates. Lay a slice of foie gras on each plate, then a potato galette, and repeat with another layer of foie gras and a second galette. The sauce is not poured over the millefeuille but around it.

Poulet Sauté au Verjus
Chicken with Verjus

THIS IS MICHEL DASSIOU'S GRANDMOTHER'S RECIPE which he liked to think would be perpetuated. Perhaps my granddaughter will make it one day. Verjus (sometimes Vert Jus) can be bought in London, but if you can't find it try using crab apples. Unripe grapes are used in the south of France; in the north gooseberries are substituted. Here is a way of making it: crush and strain 1.5–2 kg/3–4 lb white grapes through a jelly bag, squeezing out every drop. Bring to the boil and simmer gently until the juice is reduced to the thickness of pourable cream. If using crab apples, pile them in a heap in the garden for several days to sweat before crushing them in a juice extractor. A spoonful can be added to either a savoury or a sweet dish. (In Italy it is called *saba* or *sava*.)

SERVES 4

1 medium free-range chicken, cut into 8 pieces
100 g/4 oz/½ cup butter
salt and pepper
500 ml/18 fl oz/2¼ cups chicken stock
4 cloves garlic, chopped   bunch of chopped fresh parsley
100 ml/4 fl oz/½ cup verjus
few green grapes
little dry white wine, preferably Bergerac

BROWN THE CHICKEN PIECES in a little of the butter in a cast-iron casserole. Season with salt and pepper. When the pieces are golden on all sides, pour in just enough stock to cover them. Cover the casserole and leave to cook over a gentle heat until all the liquid has evaporated. Allow the juices to stick slightly to the bottom of the pan. Remove the fat with a spoon. Return to a high heat and deglaze with the rest of the stock. Add the garlic and parsley. Allow it to reduce by half, then add the verjus together with some grapes.

Remove the chicken pieces. Reduce the sauce further, adding a little wine, then whisk in a little butter, cut into small cubes. Check seasoning and serve immediately. This dish goes well with a fricassée of *cèpes, pommes sarladaises* (potatoes cooked in goose fat), or with fresh salsify sautéed in butter.

Pescajoune
Baked Apple Crêpes

I F YOUR FRYING PAN (skillet) is large enough, cook one Pescajoune; if there is too much batter cook several crêpes.

SERVES 4
4 tbsp flour
2 eggs
½ glass groundnut oil
1 glass milk
apples or pears, peeled and cored (see method)
½ glass Calvados

H EAT THE OVEN to 200°C/400°F/Gas Mark 6. Make the batter from the flour, eggs, oil and milk. It should be slightly thicker than ordinary batter.

Roughly chop the apples or pears and add to the batter. (The quantity of fruit should be equal to the amount of batter.) Heat a little oil in a flat ovenproof frying pan (skillet) and pour in the batter. When the *pescajoune* has cooked on the underside, turn it over.

Remove the pan from the heat and transfer to the oven for 30 minutes. Shake the pan lightly to loosen the *pescajoune*. Heat the Calvados in a ladle, pour over the *pescajoune* and ignite to flambé. Serve warm.

Chapter IV

A
SPOON
WITH EVERY
COURSE

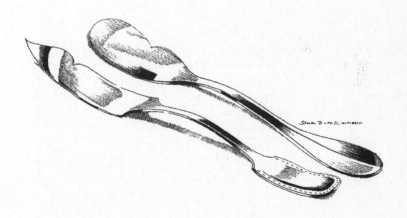

Normandy

Chapter IV
Normandy
A Spoon with Every Course

I͟T͟ ͟H͟A͟S͟ ͟T͟O͟ ͟B͟E͟ ͟S͟A͟I͟D͟. No one goes to restaurants in France for the pleasure of their décor. To eat? Certainly. But keep your eyes down. For those sensitive to their surroundings, who are looking for the complete experience, who judge a restaurant by its appearance – the lobby, the chairs, napery, lighting, pictures, curtains, and so on – must give up, turn away. Or else stay at home. Nothing would persuade a couple we were once travelling with to cross the threshold of a village restaurant which, during the year since Michael and I ate a superb meal there, had been done over. Our friends were so distracted by the glitzy door and a glimpse beyond of fanned napkins in oversized glasses, that they aesthetically gagged, backed out, and no protestations of ours could convince them that the food might be unrelated to the décor.

British *salles à manger* come nowhere near the ingenuity of naff French décor, so remarkably ugly that you cannot believe that somewhere, sometime, a person actually sat down with paper and pencil to design that flower pot in the foyer. Where in God's name does this stuff come from? And why is it still being made? Who thinks up those picture frames? What restaurateur chooses them? Who is still saying, Yes! to that patterned, sick-coloured carpet?

No doubt there'll come a day when all this tacky detritus will be auctioned off, if not at Sotheby's as invaluable *fin-de-siècle* artefacts, then in Paris flea markets as curious relics of an impoverished era. Will those grotesque ceramics standing on the bar be coveted as eagerly as I mourn the passing of heavy steel cruets with their cut-glass bottles? In the meantime it's prudent to anaesthetize visual sensibilities, ignore tacky incontinence, and merely trust to your nose.

One sign on entering a restaurant which, on more than one occasion, has been indicative of the meal to come is the napkins.

Damp ones. As at Clotilde's in the Chartreuse, where her younger sister, Angèle, was feverishly trying to finish the ironing by mid-day, damp napkins seem to testify that not only the napery but the food itself is fresh. Another clue is sauce spoons: additional shovels, lying alongside the knife, which are shallow enough to scoop up the sauce in places where they don't expect you to use bread to swab round the plate. This is most apparent in Normandy where, recklessly, you may be supplied with one of these crucial spoons for every course. Sauces are served with everything: not only coloured *coulis*, but creamy sauces often with an added thread of Calvados which lingers deliciously on the tongue.

If you arrive in Normandy via Dieppe and the timing is right, try a fishy lunch at Marmite Dieppoise or Au Grand Duquesne. Both are around the Église St-Jacques. And because four different people we'd asked in shops and at the fish stall in the market – after a certain amount of discussion among themselves – had advised us to go to the latter, we did. The restaurant, specializing in fish, is run by the Hobbé family – a son and his parents. They buy their fish at six in the morning, and are back by eight in time to make their own bread and rolls. Many of the punters were locals, spending their luncheon vouchers on one of the 'suggestions' for that day: *poêle de langoustines, tagliatelle au saumon fumé et oeuf poché, roulade de merlan au basilic* or *trançon du turbot aux cèpes frais*. Tempting as they sounded we chose *escargots au beurre d'ail* and *soupe de poisson maison*. Both were good. The soup, the colour of sandy bricks and served with dishes of mayonnaise, grated cheese and small rounds of toast, was thick and still had fragments of shell in it. We learnt afterwards that they pound the fish, but don't strain it, hence its texture. A salad dressed with walnut oil came with the grilled tails of *langoustines*; the turbot had a cream sauce with mussels and fresh tarragon, tiny black Horns of Plenty and a mound of grated celeriac folded into *crème fraiche*. The chocolate truffles brought with our coffee were as smooth as velvet and homemade in spite of the restaurant being opposite a *chocolatier*.

With the gutsy prospect of pastoral Normandy ahead of you, with all its rich, creamy, cholesterol-laden promises, Dieppe isn't a bad start for any traveller heading that way.

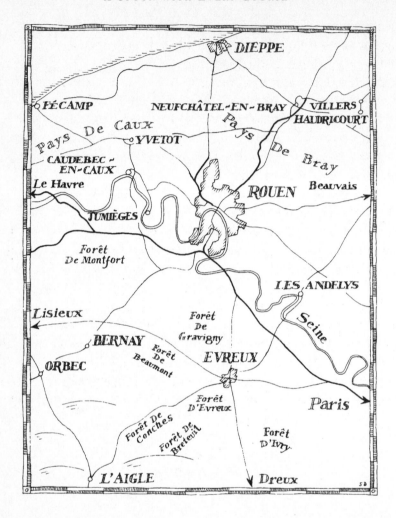

ON A SUNDAY IN SEPTEMBER my daughter Tamsin and I ate lunch in the village of Orbec. Quite unintentionally we were travelling with her youngest daughter, Meriel, a baby of three months. I don't mean that the baby being there was an absent-minded gaffe but, like the last time Tamsin accompanied me to France, to search for French gardens, we then had her first baby with us, and now, again, we were travelling with another daughter. Babies can be an asset. They slow you down, certainly, but they do cut through Gallic reserve, and not one chef refused to let the three of us come into his kitchen or appeared unwilling to sit down with us under the trees. We did discover one thing: breast-feeding in France seems so outmoded that when Tamsin retreated to the car if the meal was prolonged, there was surprised reaction to such a quaint way of feeding a baby.

Au Caneton, in the narrow street of Orbec, gives out all the right signals. (As long ago as 1960 Elizabeth David mentioned the restaurant in an article in *Vogue*.) The exterior of the seventeenth-century building is unpretentious, not plastered with awards and honours, crowns, stickers and stars. We'd been told of it by the owner of a near-by one-star establishment who (unlike the chef at Sousceyrac, who when asked where he and his wife would choose to eat in the Périgord, had replied emphatically, 'Nowhere!', which says everything about that region) had no such professional reticence. He praised Au Caneton for its use of local food. And here lies the difference. Where tourism has been seeping in for years like a parochial pollutant into certain *départements* of France, out-of-season restaurants go dead. They leave a trail of unlovely pizza places along the banks of rivers or in villages too picturesque for their own good. Yet Normandy, somehow, has still retained its intrinsic cuisine. Hence the promising extra spoon beside your plate.

Au Caneton
Un Grand Timide

WHILE TAMSIN AND I WERE READING the menu in the long, darkly-beamed dining-room with a fire burning at one end, we drank ice-cold Pommeau. The drink is not unlike Pineau de Charentes (made from fresh grape juice and Cognac), while Pommeau is made from two parts cider to one of Calvados. In the last twelve years production of the *perfumé*, slightly cloudy Pommeau has been revived. The cider used is fizzy *cidre bouché*, which is held down by a clamped cork; the other kind is flat, the 'hard' cider, that can become exciting if you assume you're merely drinking apple juice. With the drink we were given hot fragments of pastry filled with anchovy and salmon (smoked on the premises) followed, for Tamsin, by oysters in their shells served with finely-chopped shallots and parsley in a light wine vinegar, and for me slices of *andouilles* (smoked tripe sausage) – a speciality of Vire – in a thin, sharpish, cream sauce with quarters of unpeeled apples lightly cooked in butter. Slabs of butter were on the table along with rolls made that morning and warm from the oven. Cream and butter, I know, are the Normandy clichés, but as they come from the cows grazing in the orchards and meadows around us, each ingredient has its own purity of flavour.

Madame Tricot, wife of the chef, talked food to us; we were adrift among roast pigeon with apple and cinnamon; wildfowl *et son jus au Pommeau*; or a 'purse' full of lobster *en feuille de brik et crème de crustacés*. In the end we chose *rognons de veau en crème de cidre*, and duck cooked in lemon, for which the chef is renowned. The slivers of duck were narrow and pinkish with a delicate trace of Grand Marnier in the sauce. It sounds an unlikely addition but was a startling change from duck with orange. Cider isn't usually drunk with a meal, except sometimes with pork, but Monsieur Tricot does use it in cooking. The mixed green salad of *mâche*, endive and a few leaves of sorrel, had a dressing of peanut oil and wine vinegar. In a salad he considers cider vinegar too strong.

The choice of oil in cooking is critical; it may vary from region to region according to the abundance of the product in a particular area, but the distinct flavour of olive or walnut, groundnut or sunflower affects the cooking. And we invariably found that chefs voiced their preferences. Monsieur Tricot prefers the blandness of groundnut oil in some cooking and salads; another chef uses walnut oil in a strong garlic sauce; others need a mixture of oil and butter to get a high temperature; but whatever they use the choice of fat or oil is paramount.

We finished the meal with *profiteroles au chocolat* and a *tarte fine aux pommes*. When it's good, a *tarte aux pommes* can be the best thing in the world. I love its homely dependability, the change of texture on the tongue from the pastry and the apples; I like the acidity of the fruit, the sweetness of the glaze, and the comforting smell and

warmth from something I want to think has only just left the chef's hands. *Pâte sablée* filled with overlapping crescents of a local dessert apple and at the last minute sprinkled with sugar for a brief moment more is infinitely preferable to a plate of fancy concoctions covered in zig-zag patterns and an infestation of halved strawberries. (There's something so mean about cutting a strawberry in half.)

Didier Tricot comes from Picardy and when we asked his wife, a Parisienne, if we could speak to him after lunch, she warned us rather endearingly that he was '*un grand timide*', so we weren't exactly prepared for the large bearded man who sat down beside us. Tricot's grandfather, he told us, had been a butcher and though he'd died when his grandson was only eight, Tricot had already made up his mind he'd be one too. But as he grew up and became more and more fascinated from watching his aunt in the kitchen, he abandoned ideas of a blood-spattered apron and set his sights on spotless white – and a chef's toque. It was at Thonon-les-Bains on Lac Léman in the Haute-Savoie – a long way from home – that he did his *apprentissage*. From there he returned to a hotel/restaurant in Rouen before coming, seven years ago and quite by chance, to the gentler pace of life in Orbec. 'Rouen was larger, busier – quite different from this place. There my clientèle was mostly businessmen.' Now they come from the surrounding towns: from Caen, Le Havre, Lisieux, 'and some even from Paris'.

Duck, not surprisingly, is the speciality of Au Caneton; not just for *foie gras*, *aiguillette de canard en papillotte*, or a whole one simply roasted in the *jus de Pommeau*, but in particular for Tricot's duck *au jus de citron*, for which he gave us the recipe reproduced at the end of this chapter, just as he scribbled it down at one of the restaurant tables. It was superb. The birds, a cross between Barbary ducks and wild drakes, are from Duclair on the Seine, where their necks are wrung, not cut. And as though to soothe our Anglo-Saxon sensibilities he added, 'There's strict government control about the way they are killed.' Dismissive of *nouvelle cuisine*, he gestured derisively about large plates with tiny morsels on them. 'A leaf, a pretty sauce – and you are left still hungry! Thank goodness the fad is passing and we are returning to traditional cooking.' Then he added as an afterthought, 'I never invent – that is, play around – but I may adapt.

I've a collection of old recipe books dating back to the beginning of the century.'

Perhaps next year the Tricots will be awarded a Michelin star. I hope so. Not only because they deserve to be, but because Didier has strong feelings for his restaurant. Without a trace of timidity he pronounced, 'We adore it! We wouldn't want to leave now for anything.'

THE CHEF AT LE CHEVAL BLANC, Caudebec-en-Caux, dressed in blue and white striped trousers and white *sabots*, was putting rounds of dough on a baking sheet when we came down to breakfast. He bakes twice a day. The rolls are brown, crusty, and quite delicious with the butter he makes out of cream from a near-by farm and jam full of chunks of blackish-blue plums. He belongs to a *confrérie* of like-minded chefs whose aim is to *'respecter l'origine et la qualité des produits de la région'*. Until four years ago he was on the move, selling meat all over Normandy, but everything changed when he discovered this deserted hotel, dirty and with a bad reputation, which he brought to life so successfully that within a year the Logis de France stuck their plaque on his wall. Like others we came across, his is the *cuisine du terroir*. And so enthusiastic did he become telling us about the area in the *pays de Caux* where he gets his strawberries, gooseberries and raspberries, his cherries, plums, apples and pears, that we decided to

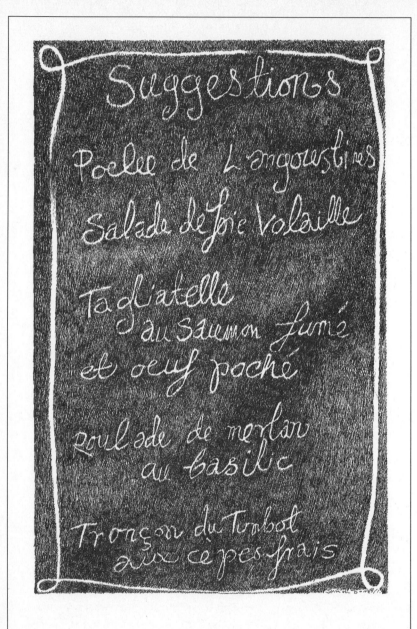

have a look at the region ourselves even though it was autumn and not as spectacular as in a blossomy spring.

In an area where the Seine twists through fertile land forming pieces as in a jigsaw, we drove along a deserted road in the valley circling the Forêt de Jumièges. Here the river, whose glassy surface appeared motionless, snakes through small orchards where the fruit and vegetables are of such high quality that the area supplies restaurants and markets for miles around. It has great charm. There is a quality of secrecy about a piece of land so fecund it forms a lush kitchen garden not many miles from the industry of Le Havre.

By 12.15pm, hungry and looking for somewhere to lunch, we chose the Auberge des Ruines at Jumièges partly because the menu for that day was handwritten and partly because, peering through the window, we saw sauce spoons already in place on the tables and that the restaurant was filling up with single men; men in suits carrying weighty briefcases, who were later joined by other men in suits with weighty briefcases. The signals were good, as promising as cooking smells and blue smoke issuing from a roadside *bistro*.

Inside we were welcomed by a Madame unfazed by a small baby and all its impedimenta. She took trouble to find us a discreet corner and later we discovered she too had a baby and knew about the problems of travel. We rejected the *Menu surprise* – that always sounds an unalluring gamble – and chose the ninety-franc menu of *moules à la crème* served out of their shells in generous bowls with a strong briny taste coming through the sauce; skate with the autumnal *trompettes de la mort* (Horns of Plenty) and deep green hummocks of spinach with a vivid *coulis de poivrons* (a red pepper sauce so delicious it needed a spoon). Neufchâtel or Livarot cheeses can be crudely strong and Pont l'Évêque I find too mild, so we chose instead the Camembert. Here in its own territory the cheese tastes nothing like those pasteurized impostors whose life has long ago been wrung out of them as they remain petrified and sterile in their circular wooden coffins. The last course was pancake cushions filled with unsquelchy apple, slightly sweetened and spicy, surrounded by *crème anglaise*. Most diners chose this menu, but at one table six businessmen, who had taken off their jackets immediately on arrival and hung them on the back of their chairs, ordered 235F menus. We watched them slowly loosen their ties, fold back their cuffs and flush visibly as between courses they gulped down glasses of *trou normand*.

Loïc Henry, the chef, spent two years at cookery school in Rouen, where each student had to '*faire cuisine et salle*' in the first year; in the second they could choose to work in either the kitchen or the dining-room. After an examination in which they both cooked and served at table, about seventy to eighty per cent received their diplomas. But schools vary. They offer a variety of courses; the one in Rouen went in for *cuisine traditionelle*, which is what Monsieur and Madame Henry have been producing ever since they worked together in Paris and Rouen before coming to Jumièges eight years ago.

We may have eaten better at other places, but the atmosphere of the Auberge des Ruines felt right and, if life works out that way, we would return for another meal. So how do you decide where to eat? What books, recommendations or gradings do you follow? Or should you trust to instinct? As far as we were concerned all these methods were fallible. Even as you read this, don't take a word of it to heart – what I may rave about with over-the-top enthusiasm may make you grind your teeth in disagreement. The enjoyment of a meal is precarious. The fishing boats may have returned empty that day; perhaps the chef has cut off his thumb or the eggs are addled; the placid Normandy cows might have the blow-fly and be gallivanting round the orchards till the milk curdles in their udders. Unforeseen setbacks can so easily throw the occasion out of kilter as happened once to us at an unjustifiably expensive restaurant recommended by a Frenchman who knew the town of Brive well. When we gave our order we were asked to choose *les desserts* at the same time – a tiresome practice that is on the increase. But having done so, it was infuriating to wait fifteen, twenty, then thirty minutes for them to arrive. When we complained, with a cursory apology the waiter acknowledged their error: the order had never gone through in spite of our premature choice. A memory like that sticks. Nothing will get us into that restaurant again, nor would I recommend it to anyone else.

Restaurant Dauphin

The Chef with the Laughing Eyes

A RESTAURANT THAT HAS KEPT its Michelin star constantly for thirty years must, surely, be worth a visit? (The *Michelin Guide*'s flaccid definition for one star is: 'A very good restaurant in its category.') The Hôtel du Dauphin is in the small town of L'Aigle, in the Pays d'Ouche, famous for years for the manufacture of pins and needles. The hotel, which used to be a *relais de poste* and have stabling for eighty horses, dates back to 1618 and even now, as soon as you push through the glass doors, there is an old-fashioned quality about it; you are aware of a shabby grandeur that is sadly vanishing from the hotels of France. Too many have that faceless modernity which leaves a traveller unable to distinguish one country from another. Here the large leather-covered couches and armchairs have not yet been replaced by synthetic furniture in curdling colours; fires burn in the massive stone fireplaces; heavy curtains reach to the floor; there are table lamps, portraits and palms in pots. This sense of timeless stability is entirely due to Roger, Jacqueline and Michel, the descendants of the original Bernards, who have kept the mirrors, rugs and panelling intact rather than introduce trendy schmaltz. Entering the sombre dining-room, divided in the centre by a magnificent Victorian counter with glass and brass lids that once held haberdashery in a draper's shop, you at once feel soothingly indulged. The service is attentive; the tables heavy with cutlery, napery, glasses and vases of fresh flowers.

The original chef in 1925, who worked for their parents for twenty-eight years, was adored by Roger, Jacqueline and Michel as children. 'The first thing I did on returning from school,' said Michel, 'was to rush into the kitchen.' They sniffed, poked and tasted everything so it was not unexpected that first Roger took over the kitchen, to be followed later by Michel. And it was under Roger that Jean-Pierre Fulep, the present chef, arriving at fourteen, did his *apprentissage* for three years before spending another three gaining wider experience in Paris.

Lean out of your hotel window on Tuesday morning and you'll discover the square below has blossomed overnight. Wafting scents and an orgy of colour are just one part of the famous weekly market that flows through the town in all directions. On the *charcuterie* stalls are *épaule de porc, filet de porc* and *poitrine de porc* to be turned into chunky *rillons* for one of the best of *hors d'oeuvres*; there are bowls of *tripe de Caen* in which minute scraps of carrot and herbs swim in a golden sea of aspic; bowls of hot *choucroute* piled into topaz mounds catch your breath with their acid fragrance; meat, fish and dairy produce – slabs of Normandy butter, better than anything you have eaten before – are alongside bowls of *crème fraîche, fromage blanc* and cream cheese. In autumn the fruit and vegetable stalls are piled high with lush purple plums as large as apples and so ripe you need only open them, remove the stone and fill each half with dollops of *crème fraîche* before baking them in an oven until the cream and juice run together in crimson streamers and the top becomes lightly crusty. *Scaroles*, as large as crocheted cushions on back windows of cars, lie among the white innocence of fleshy leeks, bundles of herbs, and rosy bulbs of garlic which, if you keep your hands off them, will last for months in your kitchen at home. In a covered market we hurried past the out-of-town vendors. Some were selling a rabbit or two, a few geese and fantail pigeons; others had a kid, a ferret or a puppy for sale. The market is so quiet; everyone seems intent on their purchasing and if it's raining, the *pavé* that runs on each side of the road glistens from the apricot, terracotta and translucent yellow of the cobbles.

'I used to work fourteen, or sometimes eighteen, hours a day at the hotel,' Jacqueline told us as we sat drinking ice-cold Pommeau

together. 'For a wedding, I'd arrive at a quarter to seven in the morning, work through till five the following morning, and then sit in an armchair for two hours because it wasn't worth undressing only to dress again!' The family keeps an eye on everything; constantly checking on the ingredients coming into the kitchen. Michel told us that once his sister has tasted a dish cooking on the stove, there's no

need for a second opinion. Michel's son-in-law is the fish expert. He buys direct from the harbour at Dieppe. Jacqueline will go into the market to choose some mushrooms for the chef, who needs particularly small ones that day; or she may go searching for the best bananas to be had, or perhaps for market poultry as an alternative to their usual supplier, a local farmer; their *charcutier*, two kilometres from L'Aigle, is the 'champion' of France for his *andouillettes*, and their *viande normande*, classed *grand cru*, comes directly from the abattoir. Bread, another ingredient painstakingly selected, was tested and rejected until they found the best source. 'We were always there to see and look at different bakers – to find the better one – to find the right one for us.' Then she added, 'Of course we have someone making pastry – we make all our own *pâtisserie*, naturally.'

Butter, cream and cheese are chosen with the same punctilious precision. 'You must get cheese from different sources because no producer can supply cheese of a constant good quality.' Some comes from Rungis to extend the range beyond the produce of Normandy and, although Jacqueline has retired from overseeing the smooth running of the restaurant, she still chooses the Camemberts. She speaks about the most famous cheese of Normandy as though they were wayward children in her care: 'Camemberts have a very tiresome temperament! My mother was extremely exacting when choosing for the restaurant.' For years they have used the same supplier but at the same time Jacqueline is prepared to try others. 'You know, Camemberts are particularly sensitive to fog, storms, cold – every variance of climate affects them!' She explained how a farmer using the same cows and the same pasture cannot be sure, even so, of getting the identical results the following week. 'I know of ten or so good makes, and yet within these makes I still need to search further to find the best batches.' When we said we wanted to visit a cheese-maker she told us of François Durand, a young man making cheese under supposedly the best atmospheric conditions possible. *'Moi, je n'achète jamais un Camembert sans en avoir tenté dix, ou vingt . . . '* Jacqueline never buys without first having tested ten or twenty, so she asked us to bring one back for her when we visited the Ferme de la Héronnière near the village of Camembert.

THE WARMTH, THE SMELL AND THE QUIET MOVEMENTS of François Durand as he made his cheeses had a soporific effect on us. We watched becalmed by the young man's rhythmic pace along the staging, one hand held behind his back, as he scooped up the unpasteurized curd and poured it into containers standing on a layer of straw. Straw and wood have a natural symbiosis with cheese. '*C'est*

le moulage à la louche' (milling with a ladle), he explained. The milk, from a herd of forty Friesian and Normandy cattle, had been standing for an hour and a half before we'd arrived that morning; by the end of the week he will have made 1,800 cheeses, their taste varying according to season and the cows' fodder. Each week his wife sells them in the market at L'Aigle, while others go to restaurants and *épiceries*, to markets and devotees who come from as far away as Paris to buy from his farm. He showed us the drying room where rows of fermenting discs lay at different stages of maturity with the date of salting and addition of penicillin written on each shelf. 'Smell, appearance and touch reveal the quality of each cheese. Those that are still white in the middle aren't ready to eat. And *ceux qui sont affinés à point, sont très crémeux.* They can't be kept.' It was a cheese *affiné à point* that Jacqueline had charged us to bring her. We did our best. And that evening in the dining-room she brought us a piece to taste. All the autumn orchards were in that fresh flavour – and it was far more gentle in taste, therefore, than one we kept to eat at home in England.

Before we left we asked Durand what effect the EC had on him. Not too much it seemed – so far – 'just little matters of hygiene and cleanliness'. But he could foresee that the problems arising from his use of unpasteurized milk (problems which will occur throughout Europe) might overwhelm him, and then we shall all lose out from such clumsy legislation.

'THE CHEF WITH THE LAUGHING EYES' is how Tamsin described Jean-Pierre Fulep after we met him in his kitchen one evening. Young, ebullient, humorous and communicative, he let us crowd into the pantry even though it was after seven. 'He never drinks, never loses his temper or his good humour,' Jacqueline told us. The atmosphere was unflurried; all the *mise en place* – the bowls of chopped herbs, shallots, etc – were there; one man had started taking orders, one was plucking a duck, another basting a piece of beef, another making an individual sauce in a small copper ramekin. And much later that evening, when all the diners had been served, Jean-Pierre was going to set off to the market at Rungis with a refrigerated van. 'I never order blind,' he said. 'I buy by taste and look – choosing each time from whichever producer has the best meat and vegetables to offer. You see, although I buy from my usual suppliers, I'm always on the lookout for others. New ones. I watch out for cost, for quality, and sometimes I hear about alternatives – better suppliers – from other people!' He smiled at Tamsin holding her small daughter, Meriel, and touched the baby's cheek.

While we talked orders were already being relayed to the kitchen from early diners; activity was hotting up, and yet still Jean-Pierre kept his cool and continued a conversation that batted along between him and Jacqueline.

'*Oui, oui*, there have been changes . . . '

'The raw liver for *foie gras* – it's going to arrive tomorrow . . . '

' . . . in particular, decoration has changed . . . '

' . . . he'll show it to you tomorrow when it arrives – raw.'

' . . . the lightness of the sauces. Much less heavy, *bien sûr* . . . '

'In this hotel we remain traditional. We introduce certain touches of originality but always respecting the sound basis of traditional cuisine.'

'A few years ago we sent everything in its dishes – the pieces of meat, the fish – everything was kept on its dish . . . '

' . . . served from hot dishes – but now it's on individual plates . . . '

' . . . there used to be *un légume* in its dish – now they're laid decoratively round the plate.'

Easier? 'No, no. For us it's much more complicated!'

And future trends?

'Trends to come? If you like, I think . . . well . . . *cuisine moderne* went over the top. It was too exaggerated with those miserable portions, the dribbles of *coulis* . . . and everything. I don't think that's for the future. I think there'll be a return to the good dishes of the past. You'll see, there's going to be a revival of traditional cooking.'

'Which we never abandoned at this hotel,' Jacqueline emphasized.

'And prices have to be kept affordable because I think that if menus are priced too high – well – one must produce quality cooking . . . but at a reasonable price.'

What major changes have taken place since he became chef? 'The tendency now is to dish up in the kitchen rather than at table. More work in the kitchen – less for the waiters!' But this method banishes for ever certain venerable specialities such as the medieval recipe for *salmis*, when the partially-cooked game was brought to the table in a *sauté* pan. The vogue nowadays is for lighter food, although *nouvelle cuisine* never took over in a big way, he explained. 'Our principle is for classic Normandy cooking, traditional menus, at a price people can afford!'

I seem to have written about the town, the market and the produce without mentioning what, actually, 'the chef with the laughing eyes' cooks. When, on our first evening at the Dauphin, drinking aperitifs of apple and peach juice liberally spiked with Calvados, we were given an oyster each, hot in its shell, lying in cream, lemon and saffron sauce, Tamsin and I realized we'd fallen on our feet. So now, to give any hungry traveller passing through Normandy an idea of what you might eat at the restaurant, here are a few things to slake your gastronomic curiosity:

Foie gras the colour of a mole's tummy, turning pinky in the centre, is made from duck liver with cognac, Porto and nutmeg. It's served

with a glass of honey-tasting Coteaux du Layon that is made from over-ripe grapes, *pourriture noble* or 'noble rot', south of the Loire where each vineyard produces its own distinctive wine.

Fricassée d'escargots cooked in butter flavoured with sharp, slightly bitter liquorice, is surrounded by coarsely-chopped spinach.

Rôti de saumon à la paysanne was unexpected in that a thick piece of salmon was wrapped around with bacon and laid on chopped carrot, cabbage and coriander leaves and a herby sauce.

Filets de sole à la normande, lightly-cooked fillets delivered straight from the coast that morning, were covered by a cream, egg yolk and lemony sauce and divided on the plate by a spine of tiny, almost black *trompettes de la mort*, scallops, mussels and prawns. The taste of sea dominated the contrasting textures from sauce and molluscs.

Fricassée de poulet fermier vallée d'Auge, which Jacqueline chooses from the market because, as she says, she needs to look and feel the chickens before deciding, is served with an unusual accompaniment

– baked apple halves filled with the gooey piquancy of melting Camembert.

While we were being served *fromage blanc* and *crème fraîche* from large earthenware bowls Tamsin muttered wisely that we'd have done better wearing dressing gowns.

Calvados ice-cream is an undreamt-of delight; here it's surrounded by hot discs of crispy fried apples dipped in fine sugar.

Even if you stick to nothing more daring than a *cassis* sorbet it appears on the plate in egg-shaped halves as dense and dark as claret.

I've never given up on chocolate. But coping with 'love-at-first-sight' – *coup de foudre au chocolat* – at the end of an excellent meal almost defeated me.

On a white plate were: a small chocolate *soufflé au Grand Marnier*; a *mousse au chocolat*; a chocolate ice-cream; and, most yielding of all, *truffe au pistache*.

They appeared as a continent of glossy, mounded, dusty and boggy browns among mahogany opulence, surrounded by hot chocolate sauce with threads of orange peel in it. And I'm not talking about the oversweet, emasculated concoctions that pass for chocolate in Britain, but the strong, bitter, devilishly black stuff which comes on with dynamic arousal.

We finished with glasses of Calvados made decades ago.

WE HAD BEEN GIVEN THE NAME of a restaurant in Normandy by a businessman in Lyon. Travelling all over France as he did, he had sifted through hundreds of bad, indifferent, over-priced and exiguous meals, so it was with a certain rising optimism that Tamsin and I decided to go to one of the places he uses when travelling in the Pays de Bray. I have already said how disappointing other people's recommendations can turn out to be. We were cautious. We decided to look in on the restaurant early and smell the air.

The air we smelt as we drove towards La Mare aux Fées was distinctly agricultural. The clayey land produces more than 180 million litres of milk and one million litres of cream a year, so no wonder, on a misty autumn morning when the stillness of the day appeared transfixed, that we were enveloped by rural pungency from a million manure heaps. Lovely. The smells of cows, pigs and horses are distinctly different from each other – unlike cats, which smell of nothing more than cosy reassurance. The sight of land where the crops have been harvested and it's too soon for workers to be about preparing for the next planting; where only a few pigeons – 'the lilacs of the feathered kingdom' – are strutting about in a desultory fashion, and the first frost has not yet brought down the leaves, has little distinction. We might have been on either side of the Channel, the landscape appeared so familiar.

It was ten o'clock when we looked in at the restaurant beside the small country lane just off the main road between Neufchâtel-en-Bray and Aumale. A fire was already burning in the dining-room; a few locals were leaning against the bar, and the proprietor was peeling carrots and leeks on to newspaper at one of the tables. From the kitchen came the homely breath of a casserole cooking. That decided it: we would come back at lunchtime.

To fill in time we went into Aumale, a pretty town of fewer than 3,000 inhabitants, with a long, tree-lined *place*, streets partly cobbled, and a hat shop filled with such confections of nonsense and practicability that it had us pressing our noses to the glass with longing for another sort of life. As I'm always on the look out for a salamander, hardware shops are where we naturally gravitate. Aumale has a splendid one. From a cavernous *quincaillerie*, with alas

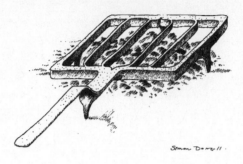

no salamander, we bought instead an iron grid – so sturdy and unchic it looked as though it had just come from the blacksmith's furnace that moment – on which to cook fish or chicken over a wood fire at home. The shopkeeper, young and loquacious, was enthusiastic when he heard we were lunching at La Mare aux Fées. 'It's good. *C'est la cuisine traditionelle*. You'll see!'

La Mare aux Fées
DAMP NAPKINS

A TABLE HAD BEEN LAID for us by the fire, where flaming logs heated a curious arrangement of water-filled pipes at the back of the hearth connected to a radiator under the window. Now and then the pipes gave off gentle sighs as if in response to the crackle of the fire. The high-backed wooden chairs had comfortable cane seats and the *vin de table* came in the customary ugly jug. Picking up the cotton napkins we were reassured to find them still damp – so damp they almost left suspicious patches on our clothes when we rose to help ourselves to *hors d'oeuvres* laid out on a table at the end of the room.

Hors d'oeuvres can be a dispiriting affair. All those things ominously cold from the fridge lying in their watery seepage and tasting of earnestly healthy eating can shrivel any lip-smacking tendencies. But we were in luck. The halves of avocados filled with vinaigrette, the haricot beans, celeriac, grated carrot and mushrooms *à la grecque* invigorated by coriander seeds, the flimsy slices of ham, a peppery terrine and pickled herrings had been prepared that morning and laid around a large pink plate of butter.

Nicole Duchossois is the owner of La Mare aux Fées and although her husband also works there, it's her name on the card and it is she who does the cooking. They've had the restaurant for thirty years – for all their married life. When Tamsin told her she'd never eaten such

delicious herrings, Nicole told us that after they were filleted and salted, they were smoked over a wood fire before being put into oil with herbs, spices and a little onion. Her *terrine de maison* is made from minced pork with seasoning, Cognac and a little water, then cooked slowly for three to four hours. '*C'est tout!*'

The *boeuf braisé* and onions in a thick dark gravy full of peppercorns, which we'd smelled earlier, was served with boiled potatoes and *choucroute*. 'I use *paleron* [chuck] that is particularly suited to braising. One can also use it – well, not nowadays, but in the past – as steak. It's very good and tender. *Très moelleuse.*' The *petit salé* is left for two months in salt, juniper, peppercorns and cloves in the *saloir* – an earthenware vat – then, rinsing it well before cooking, Nicole told us, she's left with delicious jelly from the bone.

Compote is a word that may well give out bad vibes – at least for people of my generation, for whom it used to be a watery bowl of stewed apples with little bits of core left in, or tough-skinned plums so sour they shrivelled my tongue and the pulp slid down my throat in a clammy avalanche. How different was Nicole's *compote*. Segments of rhubarb mixed with diced apples and small chunks, not slices, of unpeeled oranges had been left overnight and then cooked, without the addition of any water, with a little sugar, very gently over a stove and stirred constantly until the juices evaporated and she was left with a dense amalgam of roseate fruit.

'I've always done traditional cooking – cooking as in the past. Things like *pot au feu, saucisses 'au soule', poule au blanc, lapin aux pruneaux, le petit salé aux lentilles* – different from the way you had it today. And sometimes just large unpeeled potatoes cooked in coarse salt in the oven, then cut in half with the flesh scooped out and mixed with Neufchâtel cheese, *crème fraîche* and chives. We've always done dishes like these.' (Oh Clotilde, where are you? Is your shade beside us, listening here as we sit talking with Nicole, just as you did to us years ago? I almost looked round expecting to see you with your purple woolly hat bobbing in agreement.) 'I get my poultry, butter, *crème fraîche*, eggs . . . locally. When I cook rabbit I go to *un petit monsieur*, who's retired, whose rabbits are free-range – eating grass and *tout ça*. I've always worked like this.'

Two *hommes d'affaires* at another table called out across the room in appreciation to Nicole as they left the restaurant. She nodded to them and went on, 'My *haricots verts* come from the garden or else from Rouen market. I make a *gratin* from courgettes. At the moment we're approaching the season for pears – little pears. I cook them in red wine which I serve with red meat – either a *pavé* or a *rosbif* – things like that.' On Saturdays and Sundays they work only for reservations. 'People know us. They come for family functions, weddings, baptisms and so on. We shut only in August.'

La Mare aux Fées is one of the few restaurants we found that is a reminder of the old France, places that Elizabeth David wrote about so vividly – accounts which never pall however often you read her. Here a traveller can stop, knowing that for the price the food will be good; the appearance and smell will be authentic and there'll be no gimmicky surprises. Nor will anyone leave unsatisfied on a freezing day in winter. No wonder the Duchossois's three sons, who have grown up nourished on this kind of cooking, have all ended up in the food business. The eldest is a *pâtissier*, the second a waiter and the youngest a *cuisinier.* (Nicole didn't use the word 'chef') who works in Compiègne.

'People don't cook nowadays – not in the young families, at least. They use microwaves and *barquettes*, those kind of individual frozen pastry boats already filled. You saw a moment ago the van of frozen foods? He stopped to ask the name of clients, for example people who work, who have farms around here. Everyone now uses *barquettes*.' She sighed deeply and shrugged. 'Twenty years ago if you went to a farmer's house and they asked you to stay, you'd find *lard* [bacon] on the table. You'd have rabbit. They'd have gardens. There'd always be something – whereas now *il n'y a plus rien*. Nothing. Everything is in the freezer or in a package.'

Tomorrow, what are you cooking? 'Ah, I have a party of military men!' she said with spirit. 'I'm going to start preparing this afternoon.' What? We were longing to know. 'To begin there'll be *une salade gourmande* – lettuce and tomato, *gésiers* [gizzards], *confits* and *magrets de canard*. A separate dressing of walnut oil, Xérès [sherry] vinegar and lastly pine nuts warmed in duck fat to sprinkle on the salad.' And then? 'Turbot. Fillet of turbot with a sauce Mare aux Fées.' She could see we were going to ask. 'That is *échalotes* and lemon juice left to simmer for a long time, then *crème fraîche* and *fines herbes* are added.' The turbot comes from a fishmonger in Neufchâtel. After that there will be grilled tournedos and green beans surrounded by strips of *poitrine fumée* and a *gratin* of courgettes. 'There'll be pears macerated and cooked in spices and red wine.'

And holidays? If you can get away, where do you go? 'To Medoc, near Bordeaux. We always go there. We know some good places to eat at Casteljaloux and Marmande!' Then, as we left, she asked, '*Là, chez vous, en Angleterre, c'est autre chose la cuisine?*'

Yes. You could say that.

Recipes

L'Aiguillette de Canard au Citron
Lemon Duck Breasts

THIS WAS A SUPERB DISH when we enjoyed it at Au Caneton. The sauce was dark – neither too sweet nor astringent – but nothing like an Oriental sweet-and-sour. Didier Tricot scribbled the recipe down so that it appears like a culinary conundrum but with Shaun Hill's amendments it's well worth a try.

Serves 4
salt and pepper
4 duck breasts
1 tbsp sugar
50 ml/2 fl oz/¼ cup wine vinegar
500 ml/18 fl oz/2¼ cups good veal or chicken stock
grated zest and juice of 2 lemons
4 tsp Grand Marnier

HEAT A DRY FRYING PAN (skillet) and at the same time heat a large roasting tray in the oven at 200°C/400°F/Gas Mark 6.

Season the duck, then seal each duck breast, skin side down only, in the hot frying pan (skillet).

As the skins brown, add the sugar and let it bubble and begin to caramelize. Pour on the vinegar.

Turn the breasts in this sweet/sour mixture. Transfer to the roasting tray and cook in the oven for about 20 minutes, leaving them still quite underdone.

For the sauce, heat the stock to boiling point, then simmer and reduce until it starts to thicken. (A teaspoon of arrowroot mixed with a little wine, then stirred into the reducing sauce will help if your stock is not sufficiently gelatinous). Add the lemon juice and Grand Marnier.

Carve the duck into thin slices (the rarer the duck the thinner the slices) and spoon the sauce around with a little of the zest.

Carré d'Agneau Roti au Vinaigre de Cidre
(from Hotel du Dauphin)
Roast Loin of Lamb in Cider Vinegar

T HIS IS A PRECISE RECIPE, simple to follow, and wholly delicious. It has a sharp delicacy as well as richness from the addition of cream. Normandy cider vinegar tends to be more 'cidery' and considerably less sharp than the bought variety in England. A little dry white wine added helps to soften sharper vinegars. Also, instead of a stock of veal bones, chicken stock or a mixture of lamb and chicken bones could be used. For the *Pommes Darphin*, Pink Fir Apples work well.

SERVES 6
salt and pepper
6 loin lamb chops, each weighing about 250 g/9 oz
butter for cooking
FOR THE SAUCE:
100 g/4 oz/1 cup shallots, peeled and chopped
100 g/4 oz/1 cup dessert apples, diced
300 ml/½ pt/1¼ cups cider vinegar
500 ml/18 fl oz/2¼ cups brown veal stock
6 tsp tomato purée (paste)
200 ml/7 fl oz/⅞ cup crème fraîche
FOR THE POMMES DARPHIN:
600 g/1¼ lb potatoes, peeled
25 g/1 oz/2 tbsp butter
about 100 ml/4 fl oz/½ cup oil for frying

H EAT THE OVEN to 200°C/400°F/Gas Mark 6. Season the loin chops. Seal and brown them in a little butter in an ovenproof pan. Transfer them to the oven for about 10 minutes, depending on whether they are to be rare or well cooked.

Meanwhile, in a small saucepan, melt some butter and gently sauté the shallots together with the apple. Deglaze with the cider vinegar. Season with salt and pepper. Reduce by half, then add the stock and tomato purée (paste). Gently cook for 15 minutes. Take off the heat and add the *crème fraîche*, stirring in a spoonful at a time. Mix well and strain through a Chinois or fine sieve. Check the seasoning. Pour the sauce over the lamb chops and serve hot.

For the *Pommes Darphin*, grate the potatoes and season. Heat some butter and oil in a small heavy frying pan (skillet) and fry the potatoes in batches. Allow them to colour before turning over and cooking on the other side.

ROGNONS DE VEAU AU BEURRE MONTÉ À LA MOUTARDE
CALVES' KIDNEYS IN A MUSTARD BUTTER

HERE IS ANOTHER SUCCESSFUL NORMANDY RECIPE which really does need the vigour of Calvados to give it an authentic flavour.

SERVES 4
3 whole calves' kidneys (700–800 g/1½–1¼ lb)
butter for cooking
2 tsp minced shallots
4–5 tbsp Calvados
salt and pepper
2 tsp crème fraîche
75 g/3 oz mustard or to taste

REMOVE THE FAT from around the kidneys. Melt some butter in a frying pan (skillet) and cook the kidneys whole over moderate heat to allow them to seal and colour lightly. Cook them according to taste: rare, pink, *à point* or well cooked. Cut the kidneys into 0.5 cm/¼ in slices and keep them warm in a low oven while preparing the sauce.

Meanwhile, gently fry the shallots in butter in a pan for a few minutes over a gentle heat. Do not allow them to colour. Deglaze with the Calvados, then season with salt and pepper. Reduce the sauce by half.

Add the *crème fraîche* to the sauce, stir well and remove from the heat. With a balloon whisk, incorporate 25 g/1 oz/2 tbsp butter, cut into small pieces, and blend in the mustard. (The mixture should have a saucelike consistency.) Season according to taste. Warm the sauce, taking care not to let it boil, and pour over the kidney slices. Serve with sautéed mushrooms and vegetables of your choice.

Chapter V

A
BARBARIAN
LANDSCAPE

Ardeche & Lozère

Chapter V
Ardèche and Lozère
A Barbarian Landscape

THE ARDÈCHE IS HARDLY AN AREA that springs to mind as a gastronomic heaven. But long ago French friends had spoken of it as a singular region, a place of wilderness and small villages, of unspoilt landscape and wild flowers. So when David, Simon and I set out, our expectations of finding rural eating there which might be a revelation of unsophisticated but genuine distinction were only tentative.

The *département* spreads south of the town of Lamastre, where the Hotel du Midi has for years been famous for its splendid cuisine. How many people after eating there would long to have the ingredients and patience to make the late Madame Barattero's *pain d'écrevisses, sauce cardinal* (still on the menu) using fresh-water pike, kidney suet, butter, eggs, milk and flour, one truffle, a mushroom, and a sauce made from crayfish that includes olive oil, tomato purée, meat glaze and saffron, wine, brandy and cream? It's not something to knock off in your kitchen in an instant but well worth crossing the Channel for, taking the magnificent road between Valence and Le Puy, lunching at the Midi in the Place Seignobos, before drifting through the rest of the day when hours dissolve into trivia.

Driving up towards Privas where cherry and apple orchards were in flower, and where on narrow terraces the vines were barely in leaf, snow had not yet melted on the hills beyond. In the early morning the frost, which lay thick in the shadows, was so severe that giant sprays of water were turned on to disperse the ice threatening the tender crops. Across the pass, trees were delicately outlined in white from last night's fresh-fallen snow.

We stayed the night at the architecturally functional but splendidly sited Panoramic Escrinet, quiet and with rollicking views southwards towards Aubenas. We ate unexpectedly well: ravioli in cheesy sauce with *morilles*; monkfish rolls in a cream sauce served with *fond d'artichauts*, mushrooms, and potatoes *à la dauphinoise* and a dish of *aubergines provençales* (the stewed pulp is fried in oil with tomatoes and garlic, and served in the aubergine skins). We finished with *mousse au café* or *cassis sorbet*. The wine was a superb Ardèche Chardonnay Louis Latour.

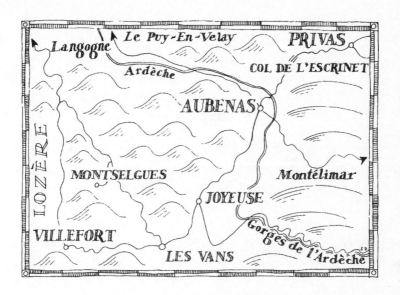

Gorges, cliffs, grottoes, rivers and pine forests; sheep, fruit trees, vines and, above all, chestnuts, seem to dominate this part of France. The much famed Gorges de l'Ardèche are a minor experience compared to other, more dramatic gorges but the grandeur of the landscape is spectacular. And the diversity of produce made from chestnuts – the liqueur, purée, *confit*, *pâté*, stuffing, soup and so on – is well worth seeking out in the larger towns.

'The autumn chill coincides with the return of chestnuts, that food of Jack Frost, the shepherds of the Ardèche and the mountaineers of Cévennes or even Corsica,' writes the chef and food writer Joël Robuchon about favourite seasonal recipes in his recent book *Cuisine des Quatre Saisons*. But sadly chestnut trees are not being replanted as vigorously as walnuts are in the Lot. This is an area where agriculture is withering. When a farmer dies his land becomes *friche* – fallow; his children have long ago escaped to the city, and who but a foreigner would consider living in such a remote region? If the abandoned property is bought, it's either as a holiday home or by some wily entrepreneur who has his sights set on making a financial killing through tourist development. But as the locals pragmatically

admit, neither the Dutch or Germans, nor the British, whether they camp or rent, will spend anything but the minimum in the local shops, preferring instead to bring their own provisions. And for the farmer who does struggle on, it only takes one seasonal disaster to finish him off.

The climate can be brutal in the mountains of the Ardèche. If a storm hurls hailstones the size of ice-cubes on an orchard of ripe cherries, the crop is annihilated. Insurance is unheard of; it's never been customary. The farmer's parents never insured, nor his grandparents before him. With a year's income lost, he's left to *vivoter*, as they say – to rub along – with a cow or two, a few rabbits, chickens and ducks. Some may still crush their own grapes, but only enough to keep them supplied for the year; some may sell a little honey, but overall the picture is bleak. The reality of such an existence reaches ironic absurdity when a couple of cows belonging to an old woman living a hand-to-mouth existence still have to be registered in Brussels.

The EC has a lot to answer for; it's changed the agricultural complexion radically. Some legislation has been beneficial, but pettifogging regulations have destroyed much to the detriment of us all, not least to French smallholders. Footling strictures from Brussels will mean a wholesale banishment of everything that makes marketing in France worthwhile. It means too that peasants with a few vegetables from their small-holdings or honey from their hives, with home-cured ham or sausages, their country *pâtés* and cheeses, will no longer set out at dawn to bring their wares to market. Regulations demanding a rigid conformity to centralized rules will result in a bland uniformity spreading through Europe from the sterility that comes from straight cucumbers and aseptic butter.

Ask an artisan who makes goats' cheese and keeps a pig or two whether his children will go on making *terrine* as it has been made for generations. His answer will be an emphatic no. Conforming to the EC regulations, made by bureaucrats abroad who have no idea of dog-and-stick farming which used to be such a great part of marginal agriculture in hilly country, has made this kind of life economically impossible. Is the Greek peasant who makes fig cakes (*sikopites*) heavily laced with ouzo and wrapped in walnut leaves, or the Italian housewife who dries tomatoes on a discarded door laid out in the sun, going to continue making these products when they are hounded by imbecilic rules thought up by people in a boardroom without a sense of priorities or of taste?

Be quick! If you are, there is still time in the cities of France to get jars of home-pickled *cèpes* from the woods of the Rouergue, or walnut *pâté*, bitter and fresh, from the autumnal harvest along the slow rivers of the Périgord, and from mountains where herds are pastured throughout the summer, dairy produce with the name of the farm handwritten on a cardboard label. I used to wonder where it originated, this food tasting intrinsically of itself without preservatives, colouring or 'clingfilm' encasing its aromatic delicacy. Who made it, and how did it get to the pavements of Lyon?

At last I've found my answer. One answer, at least, in the form of sixty-year-old Monsieur Sully, a short man with a crown of white hair brushed forward, a gnomish face, no neck and woolly ears. In fine weather he wears a checked shirt with wide braces holding his jeans up to his armpits. Except for two years in the army he's never left his area of the Ardèche where he worked as the fourth-generation cook

in the family restaurant and *épicerie*, and the second-generation baker. He had no time for children or travel, and he only started up his own restaurant because, as a baker, he had to rise so early. He rose at one in the morning to bake the bread; when that was set going he prepared fifty lunches, and then took forty winks before opening up the bar and grocery store. His knowledge of mushrooms is well-known; he's the local identifier of fungi but you'd have to be desperate to take Sully's advice to eat raw rabbit's brains as a remedy for mushroom poisoning.

Like Clotilde his reputation for generous helpings of gutsy food grew; news rippled out and clientèle from miles around came for his cooking, until he boasted that it was necessary to book a week in advance to be sure of a table. Customers came from as far away as Valence, though never from Alès, because there he had an understanding with a colleague serving the same sort of food in the Cévennes that they wouldn't poach each other's territory. Sully was famed for his *sanglier* (wild boar), that delicious gamey meat best eaten young and much sought after by hunters. Fierce as they appear, the beasts are herbivores, roaming about woods and feeding on acorns or other nuts on their migratory search for food through the Massif Central, the Pyrenees and the Alps. Sully's recipe for wild boar is a *daube*, braised in a red wine stock with plenty of herbs and seasoning. Rabbit, hare and an excellent *coq au vin* are some of his other specialities and occasionally a trout from one of the streams, but as he says, 'You can't be served a banquet on trout.' Sea fish are out. He maintains he's too far from the coast for fish to be fresh enough to taste good. What he does like doing with his hands is making charcuterie, strong, spicy and fatty, in contrast to his other passion for sauces and highly shiny fruit tarts.

Every Wednesday Sully closed the restaurant. That was the day for his bread round. *En route* he'd pick up any cheeses, butter, mushrooms, bilberries or wild raspberries from the mountain peasants and outlying farms; the sort of produce that you can still buy from stalls under the trees along the Saône at Lyon and which I shall forever appreciate now that I can imagine a thousand Sullys doing their rounds through the isolated smallholdings of France. Nowadays places like his are hounded by redtape; a few years ago Sully was closed down for serving game illegally and he never intends to open again. A similar story was told to me by a financier from Marseille, who said that he and his business cronies go into surrounding mountains, up a road going nowhere, for the pleasure of eating game. But unless they use the current password, no one can cross the threshold.

Bureaucracy has changed the pattern of life for Sully. In the old days when guidelines were more pliant it was the postman who, primed with a drink and a gossip, delivered bread and groceries from Sully's shop along with the mail before climbing the meandering mountain road. The rings are still in the street wall where, before the postman had a van, he used to tie up his mule and cart outside Sully's. Since he was closed down, and missing the friendly sociability of his restaurant, Sully comforts himself by acting as news vendor to the locality by going to Les Vans each morning and reporting on births, marriages and deaths as well as bringing back bread to the village.

In honour of friends who live in the district Sully laid on dinner for fourteen people, to which we were also invited. The long dining-room was reached by a flight of steep outside stairs (he never serves food outside, even in the summer, because, as he says, '*l'escalier c'est mortel*!', though some more vigorous friends do prefer to collect their own food to eat under the contorted limbs of a mulberry tree). The room was unadorned except for an ugly dresser filled with every drink imaginable; on the wall hung a boar's head, a cuckoo clock, along with three others which weren't working and a barometer hanging upside-down. Plastic cloths decorated with fir cones, pomegranates, birds and nuts covered the tables. Sully laid paper on ours and placed bottles of red wine – replenishing them the instant one became empty.

If we'd known what was coming we certainly would have been more forbearing in helping ourselves to the *hors d'oeuvres*: thick slabs of ham and salami slices with good bread, followed by pots of pork *pâté* substantial enough to keep one going on a day's march. The men in the party felt too constrained to bring out their clasp knives, a custom that is still perpetuated by country people from one side of France to the other. Women aren't supposed to do it, but I do. I have my own clasp knife with a horn handle and a blade worn thin through years of sharpening on stones in outlandish places.

As bottle after bottle was passed down the table the convivial decibels mounted into a crescendo as Sully appeared with the next

course, a white basin filled to the brim with sliced *cèpes* braised in oil. His cheeks glowed, he urged us on, bringing in an unending supply of bread for swabbing up the juice from the mushrooms. Not until our plates were spotless did he bring in his *chef d'oeuvre* – a hill of wild boar chunks rising from a moat of rich, dark sauce. While we ate he stood at the end of the table chatting, watching for any malingerers as

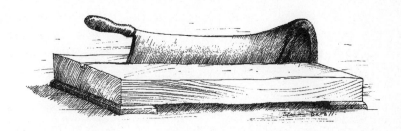

though we were recalcitrant children being picky over our food. We sighed, we groaned, we pushed back our chairs, we loosened belts, took a deep breath and then helped ourselves to *la flèque*, a regional name for potato wedges cooked in oil and water with green olives.

We staggered through a variety of beautiful white cheeses on our way to the grand finale: a series of desserts. One would have been enough, but Sully, no doubt thwarted by the enforced closure of his restaurant, wasn't going to pass up a chance of sending a salvo of puddings down the table. He surpassed himself. First came two shiny tarts of mixed fruit arranged in brightly coloured patterns; next a tray toppling with doughy fried *oreillettes* under a snowfall of icing sugar; and best of all – a classic pudding that takes a lot of beating when it's really well done – *îles flottantes* drifting in a rich, creamy yellow custard with the surface of the white-of-eggs deliciously caramelized.

The meal lasted for hours; a bit of greenery would have helped the courses along, but we'd noticed how seldom in this area fresh vegetables were on the menu. In a country where the weather is harsh, the living hard, nourishing food is a priority and delicate bits of salad in a dressing count for nothing. We'd also noticed that more than elsewhere the Ardechois spoke proudly of their traditional recipes such as *aïgo boulido* made from garlic, slices of bread and olive oil, or *alose en daube* made from shad.

Long may the Sullys of France survive by cocking a snook at EC regulations. In markets of the Ardèche vendors are still selling their cheese at the edge of pavements from baskets lined with leaves. Unwrapped honeycombs ooze their sweetness among pots of honey

made from acacias, chestnuts and *garrigue* (scrubland), or for the less discriminating, 'all the flowers of the mountain'. Among the variety of salamis lying in woven baskets were the curiously named 'Jésu', somewhat repellant and as fat as puffballs. Cluttering up the fishy quarter were fillets of salmon, little boxes of herrings and live trout in a tank. And salamanders? Where better than in the town of Aubenas to find some elderly person who might know where salamanders were lurking? Yet in spite of Simon making a sketch of one, which was passed from hand to hand, we received nothing but dusty answers. Even an ancient man in his ironmongery called 'Rome' at a crossroads in St-Ambroix, where we'd been advised to try, shook his head. He could sell us wedding kitsch or Limoges knick-knacks, even a *bain-marie* buried at the back of his shop because nowadays every sort of classic sauce can be bought ready-made in supermarkets.

What a loss. Not only for the gadget but for its name. The harmonious cadence of saying 'salamander' or 'mandolin' (another vanishing species) is forfeited while we're left with merely plodding nouns: 'grill' and 'grater'.

Restaurant La Clède
A Trace of Tamarind in the Lozère

To the south-west of the Ardèche is the Lozère, 'the lonely and lovely Lozère, the most appealing, the most quirkish, the most extraordinary of any French department I know,' wrote John Ardagh.

We'd come to the village of Villefort, to the Hotel Balme and its restaurant La Clède, on the advice of friends living in the district. We were lucky. As Villefort is a summer mountain resort, by coming out of season we missed the annual migration of healthy ramblers and charabancs full of visitors. And as the 600 or so inhabitants appeared to be indoors we had the village to ourselves.

The hotel is substantial, rooted to the ground by a solid balustraded terrace; there's a feel of bourgeois dependability as you enter. Immediately inside the tiled entrance hall, on a shelf by the door, stands a pair of quite bizarre boots. Their serrated spikes, four inches long, look fiendishly lethal, more suitable to the Chamber of Horrors at Madame Tussaud's than a country inn. But their use is entirely benevolent. They are *las solas*, used for husking chestnuts (in the south-west of France wooden scissors, with sixteen-inch jagged blades, are employed for the same purpose) which are dried in the *clèdes*, the small stone buildings you see everywhere scattered about this part.

A glass door leads out of the hall into a high-ceilinged *salon* with padded armchairs and an embroidered picture of a sailor. These hotel parlours are worth a pause, their detritus providing bits of hotel history curling at the edges as the years pass but remaining in place until they are jettisoned in favour of a stylish lobotomy. Here old menus of 1918, 1936 and 1941 sent shivers of nostalgic hunger for the days of eight or nine courses, some consisting only of vegetables. I know I go on about the paucity of vegetables, but I rage when chefs offer coloured threads of finicky decoration (a trend unforgivably perpetuated on TV food programmes), instead of taking seriously one

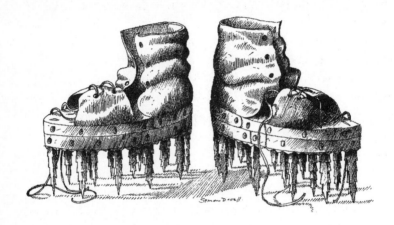

of the supreme and most versatile ingredients in cooking. To hell with the adulation of carnivores and their lust for blood: pray instead for vegetal luxuriance and bumper crops.

Opposite the *salon* is the dining-room, airy and clothed in pink. Pink radiated from tablecloths and artificial flowers, banishing the cold grey light which pressed in at the windows on the day we were there. From five different menus, each looking good, we chose salmon mousse with tomato sorbet; a *foie gras* flan with a coulis of smoked chestnuts; and snails, meadow toadstools, and buttered white nettles (they taste like sorrel) to precede *baudroie*, angler-fish, whose firm, lobster-like tail was accompanied by scallops with preserved tomatoes in olive oil; thin slices of duck breast fanned out on the plate and flavoured with spices and cranberries – not so much a sauce, but a mound of the fruit, each berry retaining its shape; and pigeon with green asparagus and fresh *morilles*, an inelegant fungus found in the surrounding woods in spring. Among the desserts was an iced soufflé laced with walnut wine.

I will not linger long on the food because I want to write about the chef. Michel Gomy is a fungi connoisseur; he uses them with enviable abandon, living as he does in a mushroom paradise. When he took us into the kitchen to show us a large cotton sack of mixed *cèpes* that a boy had just brought for the dinner that night, he impetuously scooped up handfuls for us to take home for our evening meal. 'Look, look, aren't they perfect? Aren't they marvellous? One can do anything with these, which surround us in every direction!' We looked, we agreed, we murmured.

The Lozère is a long way from Paris, where Gomy grew up. As a child watching his mother in the kitchen, learning to taste and helping her to prepare dishes, his future was cast. He knew without doubt he'd grow up to be a chef. 'From the age of ten I knew that would be my destiny.' From the *lycée*, he went into a hotel school in Paris; acquired his diplomas in three years; did compulsory army service and then launched himself into his career by working in a restaurant in the Champs Élysées and has never looked back since.

But the Lozère? Why here? Why to a part of France with the lowest population anywhere in the country? 'Well, Micheline and I came once on holiday. During our stay we spoke with Madame Balme, the proprietor, who had owned this hotel for forty years. "I'm tired now," she told us, "I want to sell my hotel and restaurant to somebody – a young couple who are in the business." We became very excited – as you can imagine!' It took them just one night of indecision. 'The next day we said OK! And that was twenty years ago.'

His is the *cuisine du terroir* – regional cooking using local ingredients – but the Lozère is poor, agriculture is running down and, for once, if it weren't for Brussels the decline would be even more headlong. Sturdy peasants with a love of their land imprinted through them, like 'Brighton' is through a stick of rock, defend their land alongside the drop-outs, free spirits, the loners, exiles or mavericks who happily find this small region bypassed by holiday touts and sun-worshipping backpackers. It's a country to escape to. Michel Gomy received forty per cent of the cost of renovating his hotel from

Brussels; elsewhere money has gone into a local trout farm and to bumping-up lamb production. 'I use all these products in my kitchen!'

Traditionally the food is heavy, as we knew already from Sully's feast, but Gomy in his loyalty to indigenous recipes does prefer to leaven it. 'For example, my calf's foot filled with chicken mousse is local cooking, but I make it a bit lighter.' He shrugged. 'And anyway, we can't eat as we did twenty years ago. Then people had to walk to the butcher, now they go by car.' Gomy's butcher is a young man, receptive and willing to go along with Gomy's innovations such as *confits* and sausages made with chestnuts. 'It's just simple things, you know, like that,' he explained. When *nouvelle cuisine* was in ascendency, he remained steadfast. 'I never change my religion in cooking.' Gomy follows the seasons, wanting to keep within their rhythmic cycle, as in autumn when there's a surfeit of wild boar that roam everywhere, even getting into gardens. And fish; what he can't get in his district comes by train from Rungis where the dealers are only too desperate to foster their small restaurateurs. 'We have six trains a day coming in this direction to Villefort.' And to prove that even a cook in the Lozère is in touch with the world he recounted how, when his chemist returned from a holiday in the Seychelles drooling over a fish he'd eaten, *bourgeois* – a snapper with a rosy-pink body with black edges to its large spiny fin and firm white flesh, and considered the best in the Indian Ocean – Gomy was goaded. He phoned Rungis, challenged them to get him a *bourgeois*, and when it came asked his friend to dinner.

Chestnuts are a major ingredient in the cuisine at La Clède. Blinis, to accompany smoked trout, are made with chestnut flour; there are beef cooked with chestnuts, chestnut cakes and a chestnut sauce. 'The basis of the food in the Cévennes for the poor people was smoked chestnut, the *bagana*, flavoured with either salt or sugar. But it's terribly heavy – quite impossible to serve in the restaurant – though my chestnut with goose isn't bad!' His belief is that anyone can make something wonderful with caviar, but to make something first-rate with lentils, say, which takes much longer and is a lot more work, that is genius. 'Anyone can put slices of factory-processed liver on a salad, you get it everywhere, and especially in fast-food places, but I try to make something that you can't find *anywhere*. Such as my calves' feet with goose liver.'

Reading his menu or unravelling the scents in the kitchen, there is an alien influence hanging round the cuisine. And then Michel explained. When a friend from the village, who worked in banking in the Far East, invited the Gomys to Malaysia in 1981, Michel was

confounded by what he found under the saucepan lids. So seduced, so in love he became with Oriental cooking that he stayed out there, working for several years in different eastern countries. When the Gomys returned to La Clède Michel brought with him a whole new language of food. Now there is always something eastern on the menu. The day we were there it was *la volaille fermière au curry Thai et riz parfumé*, and a *gigotin d'agneau* spiked with the juice of tamarind and mace.

If a quarter of his food is south-east Asian, it is for people from the surrounding towns. 'It's not for those from Paris, Belgium, Britain – they come for *cuisine du terroir*. They want local food and local wine – that doesn't come from the Lozère, because we don't have any – but some of the Languedoc-Roussillon wines.'

So intense is his love of native food that he and an equally partisan eater started up the Peyroulade brotherhood: its primary objective being to promote and to flaunt local produce. A framed drawing shows members of the Confrérie de la Peyroulade, dressed in long blue robes with yellow bands round their hats, at the *cérémonie d'intronisation* (enthronment) on Thursday 7 August 1986. Gomy, tall and imposing, is offering a spoonful of soup to an initiate, who looks somewhat cowed at the prospect. 'We had the *confrérie* around our barley soup! It's an old soup from the country here. Potatoes, leeks, smoked ham, sausage and pearl barley.' The next year the soup was served at midday along the streets of Villefort and for the year after they considered following the soup by *flaouzouno*, a Cevenol dessert made with *tome de chèvre* on a base of *tarte sucrée*. His fervour showed that the whole procedure was taken very seriously and involved endless huddles over meals to discuss the next year's ceremony.

As we carried away our mushroom booty, Gomy said with a benign smile, 'I'm very proud! When we bought the hotel and renewed the façade, we wanted to keep the old style so that when you opened the door you have to feel there is a story to the place.' Before we left he remarked, 'The first thing I do every morning is to open the window to see the mountains because – you know Paris? – in twenty years it's changed and not in a good way. But here – ah, it's a good life!' Then with a hungry glitter in his eye he added, 'We have a lot of friends coming tonight – to eat *morilles* with a big capon.'

CHEZ CLOTILDE HAD BEEN MY LODESTAR for this whole quest. Would we ever again find such a place as hers in the remoteness of the Chartreuse, where time remained spellbound around the cooking pot, and gadgets had not yet changed the pace? It seemed unlikely. After all, our knowledge of Clotilde ranged back through decades when we had traversed and re-traversed the route between Greece and England, choosing different frontiers, tunnels, passes and coasts to make the journey, but being drawn back inevitably every few years to Clotilde's door. Every traveller knows the dread of returning to a place where they have eaten well. Favourite hotels and restaurants have an almost mandatory fate for being face-lifted. The modernization is always to their detriment, whether in the new annexe to a *pensione* in Florence, the Oriental Hotel in Bangkok, or a country inn with its ugly, glass extension where the discerning traveller knows, when booking, to ask to be housed in the old part and not in the new bedrooms overlooking the swimming pool.

On the day we set out to find Chez Francine, we'd no idea that another Clotilde existed at the end of a long road. Friends, though they hadn't eaten there themselves, had heard of her existence and kindly made a reservation for us. Francine needed two days' notice. Living in such a remote area meant that she had to go to market to stock up on fresh food if she was to give us the meal she would like to present, rather then depend on eggs, potatoes and homemade *cochonnailles*.

On our way we stopped in the fortified town of Joyeuse, with stalls on a street running downhill to the main market, dark pines growing around the ramparts, and narrow houses with iron balconies where the black trunks of leafless vines snaked up from floor to floor. The cheese dealer, Michel Theron, and his wife tour the region and this was their day in Joyeuse. With such a choice of local goat and ewe cheeses, some no bigger than cotton-reels, we would have dithered endlessly. Friendly and helpful, he was willing to spend time advising us which cheeses would be suitable to put into jars of olive oil invigorated by herbs, garlic or lemon peel to take back to England. But be warned! At home I kept my jars in a kitchen cupboard. When I

came to use them three months later, the jars opened with a fizz; the cheeses had fermented; down the drain went the olive oil, herbs and all Michel Theron's delectable little cheeses as a result of my monumental stupidity and to my unabated chagrin. David, wisely, had stored his in a cold pantry.

We did turn our backs on *yaourt aromatisé*, delightful as it sounded, and on the renowned Cantal – one of the best cheeses, with a lively trace of minerals about it when it hasn't been bludgeoned into blandness from pasteurization and impatient maturing – a cheese, so Theron told us, that was the oldest; it had been produced in the Auvergne for more than 2,000 years. Picodon de l'Ardèche is a round goats' cheese and one we particularly liked, smooth-textured, mild and nutty. But best of all is Beaufort made from the milk of cows grazing among the flowery pastures of the Haute-Savoie and Haute-Tarentaise. It's used in *tarte au Beaufort* made with *pâte brisée* and ham. Or it goes well with a salad of scarole, batavia and lettuce, or in an omelette with *crème fraîche* and herbs. Large, half-cut discs of hard cheeses were protected from drying out by red and white cotton napkins, and ranged among the display were bottles of wine suggestively forcing the purchaser's pace. In reply to my question as to whether any of his children were interested in becoming an itinerant cheese vendor, he told us that his daughter wants to be a hairdresser, preferring that her hands smell of shampoo rather than rennet. She had been to England, he proudly told us, on an exchange with a girl in Birmingham, and had adored it. '*Elle est tombée* into a family there and loved every moment.'

The fishmonger, Poissonier Alonso, was a young man from Aubenas. His stall promised that his produce came straight from *des Ports Océan et Méditerranée*, and that his *produits de la mer donnent une santé de fer* (guaranteeing that his produce would give you a constitution of iron). How could we resist such tempting pledges? As the nearest sea is about two hours' drive away, unless he's there at the opportune moment the best of a catch is sent directly to the large hotels or to Rungis in Paris. Wearing a dark blue cotton smock he presided over a collection of shellfish: whelks, cockles, scallops, mussels and oysters with their range of names, one, which always seems to me somewhat capricious, *violet*. Among the roes, smoked sprats and bright-eyed, glistening fish were rosy *dorades* so beautiful no wonder they were sacred to Aphrodite. Alonso handled them tenderly, stroking every fish as he placed it on the scales, and wrapping each one up with such care that he appeared almost reluctant to let it leave his custody.

We wandered on in a bemused state of enjoyment that any foreigner, at least from Britain, feels when dawdling through a French market. Here you can still find stalls that sell those sleeveless flowery overalls, made of pure cotton, which have been in markets ever since I can remember. I used to bring them home vainly hoping that by wearing one I would somehow take on the attributes of a French housewife, not just in appearance but in culinary dexterity.

Leaving the market, we passed a pile of exceedingly tough black boots lying on a blanket on the ground, indicative of the rough and shaly terrain that we were about to encounter on our way to lunch. It's a landscape seemingly made up of outcrops of rocks and shale, with barely any topsoil in which to plant a seed but plenty of material for those gardeners who go in for alpines and stone terracing.

Somewhere *en route* to Francine we stopped in a church. A jam-jar of scarlet tulips stood on the altar beside another full of lilac, irises and wild garlic: a touching sign because, although the church is invariably empty, here was a tangible legacy of an absent human being. Someone had brought in the flowers, found water, and arranged them as a small gesture of homage. When we left a few snowflakes were falling and quince trees in flower appeared incongruous in such a wintry scene, where the wild hellebores in the woods drooped their heads even more furtively than usual at the unseasonable and inclement weather.

Chez Francine
Cuckoo Snow

S NOW AT THIS TIME OF YEAR is known poetically as the *neige de cuckoo*; and snow covered the mountain tops. The electricity wires that spanned deep ravines and valleys in vast droops must have utterly changed the pattern of living for many villagers and lonely farmsteads when first installed. As we drove up the mountain towards the hamlet of Montselgues the world became greyer and more lonely. Spring was struggling to take over, but few birds sang and only on banks sheltered from the prevailing wind was there a sign of green vegetation among the pines. When we arrived not a person was about and the place was silent, wrapped in a wintry scene of complete suspension. The notice for the restaurant was obscure; fastened to the wall of a house, in the leaden light of midday it was almost indiscernible. We turned into a farmyard. A low stone building, with no indication of what it was, had shabby brown shutters and, on either side of the entrance, a jumble of oil cans, baskets and stone querns holding a few crouching plants.

We pushed open the door and entered a low beamed room about twelve by sixteen feet. Apart from a serving table in the window five solid wooden tables filled the space, empty but for two men talking

139

together in the corner. A fire was burning on a raised hearth under a large mantelpiece and fire irons, fallen like giant spillikins, lay sprawled in the cinders. Standing on a trivet was a large and blackened pot; more pots, made of clay, stood on the far side of the hearth. From the rough-cast walls hung a cow bell, a calendar, a string of garlic, a storm lantern and various oil lamps (the electricity goes off in a high wind). Against one wall a cupboard stood open. Inside were shelves of glasses, bowls and crockery, the white sort that can still be found in markets, and centred among the shelves, a drawer for cutlery. The shelves were bordered with crocheted cotton lace edging and a lace curtain covered half the glass of a door into the passage.

Francine Foure, wearing pebble spectacles and flowery trousers, was small; she shuffled across the floor in bedroom slippers to welcome us and lead us to the table by the fire, already laid with a basket of bread and a jug of wine. She'd been waiting for us; so I think had the two men, because immediately a large earthenware tureen, filled with thick soup made from barley, potatoes and onions, from which we helped ourselves, was then passed over to the other table. The nourishing warmth of the soup was as benevolent as a hot-water-bottle in a damp bed.

Francine, who learnt to cook from her mother, is scornful of today's fad for fanciful cooking, for the elaboration and visually fiddly arrangements to the detriment of taste. As she says, 'I don't want to go in for *quelques trucs*!' (tricks, knacks, dodges). The second course was radishes and *pâté* served with a large block of butter tasting suitably bovine. 'I make the *pâté* once a year from pork, lard, an egg, herbs of Provence, juniper and cognac.' The right ratio of fat to pork preserves it well.

What followed next was as surprising as once being offered Ovaltine in an outdoor café on the borders of Burma and Thailand. Somehow, in that earthy setting, with the rough floor, smell of wood smoke and snow falling outside, we had not anticipated eating anything as fragile as the hot tarts Francine brought to table. The crumbly pastry shells were filled with bacon and mushrooms covered in an eggy sauce. The savoury taste and creamy texture in contrast to

the delicate pastry was something belonging to dining-rooms full of white napery and discreet lighting. We ate two each.

By now Francine's pets had joined us. The dog Boulette curled up under the table making a warm mat for our feet, and the cat Bibi, a sort of squashed-prune colour, sat purring between Simon and me. *Gratin dauphinois* with a crispy lid seasoned with thyme came

straight from the oven to the table so scalding that Francine put the dish down on a block of wood and then brought in a plate of small lamb chops, tender, sweet and pinkish, cooked in the oven in butter and herbs. It was too much for Boulette; frenzied by the exciting smells he thrust his muzzle up at us and every time Bibi, who was by now on Simon's lap, spat at him and gave him such vicious blows across his nose that momentarily he withdrew.

Every now and then one of the men would get up to revive the fire by blowing down a hollowed piece of wood where a jutting branch had been fashioned into a handle. This one had been well used – it was about eighteen inches long and charred at the end, but when new they're over two-and-a-half feet long. Mine is at home; I haven't had it many winters. When we asked one of the men where he worked, he shrugged, and somewhat cryptically replied that he did a bit of this, a bit of that: '*Alors*, one has to eat a little of each trade to live!' From under a wickerwork dome standing on a table Francine brought us some locally-made goats' cheese and followed it by serving each of us with a slice of apple flan, including one for herself, which she ate with the men at their table. The pastry, made from chestnut flour, was thin; a mixture of eggs and sugar had been poured over the sliced apples and the whole concoction had been baked to the colour of Demerara sugar. Until the last course we'd kept the same utensils and plates, as we'd done at Sully's and *chez* Clotilde.

While we drank our coffee from cups without saucers, we could see the snow outside falling so thickly that the view across the yard was concealed by swirling flakes. It was easy to imagine how marooned life must be up here for months at a time. And this was April! Yet, before we left, Francine picked me a sprig of olive from a tree she cosseted in a corner of the yard: a reminder perhaps of her sultry homeland in Provence.

As we descended the mountain through lessening snow until the land appeared green and the wild heights were left behind, I thought once more of Francine's persuasive words as she gave me the piece of olive. Looking at me intensely as we shook hands she said, 'You must not destroy the olive before next Easter.' Now at home her sprig, with whatever prophetic magic it carries, hangs inviolate above my bed.

Recipes

Estouffado de Sanglier
Wild Boar Estoffade

WILD BOAR IS HUNTED in the Ardèche, almost obsessively, from September to New Year. The better cuts of meat are roasted but a favourite meal is this hearty stew ('estouffado' or daube), preferably accompanied by a potato dish with green olives (*flèque*). The recipe works just as well with a piece of flank or shoulder of venison as an excellent, substantial winter dish.

SERVES 6
800 g/1¼ lb lean wild boar, cut into large cubes
about 1 tbsp lard (shortening)
2 onions, peeled and roughly sliced
1 clove garlic, crushed
1 tbsp flour
FOR THE MARINADE:
2 onions, stuck with cloves
3 bay leaves   6 peppercorns
2 cloves garlic, crushed
2 tsp dried thyme   fresh parsley sprigs
1 bottle (75 cl) red wine
2 tbsp olive oil

MIX THE MARINADE INGREDIENTS and stir in the cubes of meat. Leave to marinate in a cool place for 24 hours. Strain the meat and reserve only the liquid of the marinade.

In a heavy pan, melt the lard (shortening) and brown the meat, onions and garlic. Sprinkle over the flour and stir well. Then add a ladle of the reserved marinade juices. Cover and cook gently for about 2 hours, stirring from time to time and adding more marinade little by little. Test the meat by pricking with a fork. If, by the time the meat is cooked, the sauce is too liquid, add a little *beurre manié* (see page 29) to thicken. Serve with mashed potatoes or *flèque*.

Petits Salés de Saumon
Lardons of Salmon with Lentil Sauce

THIS RECIPE OF MICHEL GOMY'S **from Hotel La Clède is easy and quite delicious. To improve on the appearance of the dish I use a sprinkling of orange zest (which isn't too overpowering), plus chopped green herbs, according to what I have.**

Serves 6
1 fillet salmon (1 kg/2¼ lb)
18 very thin smoked bacon slices
100 g/4 oz/½ cup green lentils
1 onion, peeled   1 carrot
grated zest of 1 orange
1 tbsp chopped fresh mixed herbs, such as parsley, chives, tarragon
200 ml/7 fl oz/⅞ cup crème fraîche

WASH THE SALMON and remove skin and bones. Cut into 18 thumb-size pieces and wrap each in a slice of bacon.

For the lentil sauce, put the lentils into a saucepan with the onion, carrot, zest of the orange and chopped herbs. Cover with cold water and simmer until tender. Drain off excess liquid. Finish the sauce by adding the *crème fraîche*, then reduce by boiling to the desired consistency.

Meanwhile, steam the salmon pieces for about 3 minutes. Pour the sauce on the plates, then place three pieces of wrapped salmon on each.

Flèque
Potatoes with Green Olives

Serves 6
1 large onion, peeled and sliced
25 g/1 oz/2 tbsp lard (shortening)
1 kg/2¼ lb potatoes, peeled and cut into large pieces
1 bay leaf   pinch thyme
100 g/4 oz/¾ cup green olives
salt

Brown the sliced onion in the lard (shortening) in a heavy pan. Add the potatoes, bay leaf, thyme and 400 ml/14 fl oz/1¾ cups water. Cover and simmer for 30 minutes until almost all the liquid is absorbed. Add the green olives and salt to taste, then simmer for a further 15 minutes.

Gateaux Marrons Sauce Chocolat
Chestnut Cake with Chocolate Sauce

The friend who followed this recipe and promised to bring me a piece said it was so delicious her children had scoffed the lot, so I never had a chance.

Makes One 20–23 cm/8–9 in Cake
500 g/18 oz can sweetened purée de marrons
100 g/4 oz/½ cup unsalted butter
3 eggs
a few drops of vanilla essence (extract)
For the Sauce:
300 g/11 oz top quality plain or couverture chocolate, grated
300 ml/½ pt/1¼ cups cream
25 g/1 oz/2 tbsp butter

Heat the oven to 150°C/300°F/Gas Mark 2. Gently melt the *marrons* and butter in a pan. When blended, remove from the heat and add the eggs, one by one. Stir in the vanilla. Place in a 20–23 cm/8–9 in buttered cake tin. Bake for 45 minutes. Leave to cool.

Melt the chocolate slowly in a bowl over a pan of warm water. Boil the cream, then allow to cool slightly. Stir into the chocolate with the knob of butter to make the sauce shiny. Serve the cake with the cold chocolate sauce.

A LAND
FOR
WANDERING
SYBARITES

Gascogne & Languedoc

Chapter VI
Gascogne–Languedoc
A Land For Wandering Sybarites

I GO MAD TRYING TO SORT OUT French provinces. The boundaries of *départements* and regions seem to slew and yaw like a ship off course. I can never keep up. For one thing it's impossible not to fall in love with words. '*Haute*' this or that does nothing for me, nor do I find that the monosyllabic Aude, Eure and Lot, Gard, Var, Aisne and Ain drop from the tongue like mellifluous nouns evoking landscapes of sumptuous wilderness. But say aloud Roussillon, Dauphiné, Languedoc. Or let your tongue linger round Limousin or Lorraine. Such words undermine any hope of keeping your head, of being sensible and, in my case, of sticking to decilitres and kilogrammes, to chefs' whims and tourists' predilections.

In this chapter I want to embrace the whole of everywhere: the strange, historic, imperishable south-west of France which I don't know well, but which even on a first visit long, long ago has remained rooted somewhere in my memory, recollected only in dreams. It's a wild country for flying over. In my sleep I drift on the thermals above ravines, soar in silence over woods, annihilating on the instant all earthly trivia. The names of rivers work like an incantation: the Garonne, the Tarn, the Ariège and the secretive river of the Aveyron which rises in the bleak Causse de Sévérac not far from the Causse de Sauveterre. 'Sauveterre': there's a word to suck on like a toffee. Bosky valleys lie between the whitening bones of limestone plateaus of the *causses* reaching down to the Cévennes.

I love these uplands for their desolation: their cataclysmic quality of being at the end of the world. The only living things appear to be *brebis* – flocks of small sheep – their backs towards the prevailing wind, grazing among juniper in a withered terrain. From such unprepossessing summer nourishment we get Roquefort cheese. A cheese whose maturity, like many others today, is often manipulated until no one 'could now be driven from a train compartment by the smell of Roquefort . . . ' Gascogne, the Gers and the Albigeois are part of this country – and I write so little – a restaurant and a market. It doesn't do the region justice. But, please, someone, I need more time.

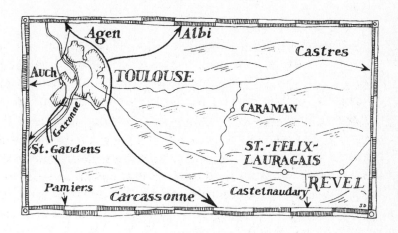

COMING SOUTH IN AUTUMN, the vines north of Cahors are turning. Some are a warm, rather than a deafening red; some have the mixed tones of stewed Victoria plums. If you bypass the centre of Cahors, with its handsome main street flanked by trees going downhill to the river, prepare yourself for a visual assault. On the outskirts, among a mishmash of commerce and roundabouts, are examples of the most outrageous municipal planting. Only a demented landscape designer high on a cocktail of propane laced with meths could have dreamt this up. They are worth a look, the roundabouts. They surpass imagination. And a twelve-foot bottle of Cahors wine made of bedding plants merits circling the roundabout for a second time. You may miss the fourteenth-century fortified Pont Valentré, turreted and noble, but what achievements of the twentieth century are lying in wait in the suburbs.

The colour of the earth towards Montauban, where the pink buildings are reflected in the Tarn, is bluish-brown, quite different to the redder colour of the Périgord. Further south, towards Auch, rows of ripe apples dangle on the cordons of orderly orchards; some, by the side of the road, are for sale, as is garlic, an essential ingredient of this region's cooking. One Gascony dish includes half a whole garlic bulb floating in a bowl of soup; another has a roasted leg of lamb surrounded by sauce made from a pound of garlic. Bring home plaits of the *l'ail rose*; in a cool place they last through the winter, never going mouldy, never impatient for spring.

South of Auch, past a gentle landscape of small hills and poplars, David, Simon and I stopped one morning when cobwebs were white with dew and creamy cows appeared ghostly on banks, to look at a forty-five-franc lunchtime menu of the restaurant in the hamlet of Ornezan in the Gers: *mousse de poisson ou taboulé*; *raie beurre noisette ou navarin de mouton*; *fromage ou dessert*. Not bad for that price – and it might possibly have been delicious. In gardens banana trees and stumpy palms appeared incongruous among pyracantha, hydrangeas and vines. Further south-west still there were autumn crocus, distant snow, shepherdesses and Spain.

And what of the produce? Some of the province's richness comes from *foie gras*, veal, hare, partridge, woodcock, pigeons and, sadly, small birds; trout and crayfish; all kinds of vegetables, including leeks, broad beans, pumpkins and chard, *chicorée frisée*, rocket and *mâche*; quince, juniper and prunes. The justifiably renowned prunes of Agen appear in many dishes both sweet and savoury, 'Prunes stuffed with *pâté* are an unusually good accompaniment to all kinds of poultry,' Jeanne Strang suggests in her book on the region, *Goose Fat and Garlic*. Honey, goats' cheeses, cassis and Armagnac are other products of the land. Armagnac comes from a small region due east of Toulouse. When cherries, raspberries or plums are macerated in this dry brandy, as powerful as Cognac but with a more vigorous bouquet, it's like holding a drunken summer in one glass. *Floc de Gascogne*, a spirited aperitif when served chilled, is made from Armagnac and grape juice; another, made from oranges marinated in Armagnac and served in a local sparkling wine, goes by the dramatic name of *pousse-rapière*. The potent drink was intended to give a final shot in the arm to a duellist withdrawing his *épée* from his prone adversary. One last word on Armagnac while we're in the region, Jeanne Strang gives a recipe I'd like to try once I've a bottle in the house, for Armagnac and kidneys: *les rognons de veau à l'armagnac*, with the addition of white wine, tomato purée, and so on plus, of course, goose or duck fat.

What of the eating – besides kidneys, cocks' combs or *cassoulet*? There are hearty recipes for rabbit, wine and prunes; for *ailicuit* – a ragout of turkey wings, giblets and gizzards with unsalted bacon and white wine; and a substantial bean soup, *l'oulade*, from the Languedoc. Refinement, purity and showy sophistication don't come into this style of cooking. In *South from Toulouse – Journeys in South-western France*, Andrew Shirley describes a restaurant in Carcassonne: 'As you read the *Carte du Jour*, your nostrils twitch to smells upstairs, and your fate is sealed . . . It was the *Confit d'oie* that did it.' He ate it with peas and bits of bacon. At Rodez in the Aveyron he describes a *terrine de grives* (thrushes) which 'tastes so light and flavoured that you know instinctively who had the soft fruit from your garden'. The butter served with the steak was blended with parsley, tarragon, chives and garlic. The garlic scented the butter – but not too overpoweringly because by then, Shirley explained, a boy had been chopping it for an hour. 'And of such are the dishes of heaven.' As for 'afters', prunes marinated in Armagnac appear in a rainbow of sweet recipes.

Going back in time from the 1950s, when Andrew Shirley was writing, the Goncourt brothers in their journal on 3 April 1878 describe a dinner party. They were guests at a house-warming of Émile Zola's (where, incidentally, Flaubert misbehaved himself by reeling off oaths and obscenities): 'He gave us a very choice, very tasty dinner, a real gourmet's dinner, including some grouse whose scented flesh Daudet compared to an old courtesan's flesh marinaded in a bidet.' Oh my! If only the wordy descriptions on menus nowadays were half as vivid we'd all order double! And I bet the grouse was delicious.

IN *LA VILLE ROSE*, TOULOUSE, there's a covered market, Victor Hugo. Outside, for almost a kilometre along the boulevard de Strasbourg, are stalls of fruit and vegetables that would tempt any traveller who had a temporary kitchen to go home to. We didn't. We had come to see the produce of the covered market and to eat in one of the small bistros on the floor above. Toulouse on the Garonne river is a sprawling provincial city. Nowadays no one can walk into the country from the old centre as they used to; the high-tech industrial suburbs, with their hideous furniture emporia, high-rise flats, laboratories and factories have spread around the picturesque centre like an expanding blight.

I was already sold on Toulouse for its association with Antoine de Saint-Exupéry. He is an author whose books I have loved for years for their sad evocation of a lonely spirit and the imperilled sanity of mankind; for his allegorical tale of *The Little Prince*, and for his books about aviation, *Wind, Sand and Stars*, *Flight to Arras* and *Night Flight*. In the 1920s he was based in Toulouse, working for the airmail delivery service. It may sound dull, but his dangerous missions in a tiny plane carrying mail all over the world; his account of flying into a viciously powerful wind coming off the mountains of the Andes when his plane was so light that it hovered perilously, suspended off the coast; his descriptions of night flying alone among the stars, all kept my mind's eyes on stalks. In 1944 he died on one of his flights: he'd left from Lyon on a mapping expedition and never returned.

The market in Toulouse was jostling and smelly; smells that worked through the sensory system at different tempos. The first, on entering the market, was one of the best in the world, redolent of comfort and friendship. Coffee. The smell was palpable, but I couldn't see where it came from. The *charcuterie* smelt of provocation, coming on strongly it reminded me of picnics and hunger; invisible gulls flew over the brackish shellfish; and the fungi smelt of aboriginal rain forests. At the stall, stretching into the distance, a man was choosing his mushrooms with fastidious care, scrutinizing each one so painstakingly that it was obvious for him shopping was not a functional necessity, but an art form, something anticipated, serious, to be lingered over. How different from those who regard shopping as a chore; who grab the first polythene bag off a supermarket shelf and flee. In French markets no one appears to be in a hurry and when you buy fish, for instance, a lemon is added to your bag; with mushrooms, it's parsley. One woman was buying a single mushroom – it weighed half a kilo. She would slice it in broad pieces, she confided to me, and fry them in oil, not butter, with garlic and parsley. Some mushrooms were orangey bits of velvet, others looked like hard-core, and some like unknapped flints. Their price varied from the *trompettes* at fifty-five francs a kilo to the king of mushrooms, the thick-stemmed ceps, at a hundred francs. Hearing I was English and seeing me spaced out

in front of the stall, a woman came up to me and pronounced succinctly, 'You must be astonished (*étonné*)!' She was dead right. David and I joined the crowd round a bar with our pieces of bread and *jambon cru* we'd had put together by the baker and I thought of our market at home, where there's a stall for burgers and tea that – for all I know – may be mouth-watering, but they've missed the point, they don't sell wine.

The pasta stall was a long ribbon of wishful thinking, with pasta purses stuffed with every sort of filling. Just to stand in front of the ravioli collection made my reason run amok: *ravioli au basilic et fromage, mini ravioli au jambon, ravioli au jambon de la Montagne Noire, ravioli à la lotte et estragon, ravioli au gésiers confit, ravioli au cèpes, ravioli gourmand 'boeuf légume'* – and we haven't reached the *lasagne*. The *saucisses* and *saucissons* were sprawled on trays like some ghastly massacre of dolls' limbs, their different coloured skins ranging from waxen to ochre. At one stall, conversing with a customer, the vendor had thrust his face so far forward through suspended sausages that his whole head was draped in them. By nightfall how well greased and spicy his cheeks would taste as his wife embraced him.

The forty-foot-long cheese stall called 'Betty' was paradise. It's no good attempting to name the choice; they came from every region from the Pyrenees to Haute-Savoie and from Brittany to Corsica, where the romantically named *brin d'Amour* (a 'sprig' of love), is made out of goats' or ewes' milk shaped into squares, covered with herbs and smelling of hay. Some were small Provençal cakes wrapped in vine leaves; some were mouldy domes; others were pillars of Fourme d'Ambert surrounded by dry little goats' cheeses easily mistaken for biscuits. Morbier, a semi-soft curd cheese, comes from the Pays de Bresse, whereas *boulette d'Avesnes*, hand-moulded with tarragon, chives and crushed cloves, and *la butte* with its *croûte-fleuri*, both come from north-western France. Every variety of ripeness was to be had among ewes' and goats' cheeses, and every range of yellows, whites, oranges and black with polished or dusty rinds. A giant Cantal cheese, the size of a footstool and weighing about forty kilos, stood on the counter, uncut. The cheese takes two years to mature and comes from Salers, a medieval village whose houses are built of lava stone and tiled with heavy slices of stone, high in the Auvergne. The staff at Betty's, who are at the Victor Hugo market every morning at 4.00 am, were willing to answer all our questions and they made a point of showing us a Stilton that their customers '*l'aiment beaucoup*'.

Fromagers affineurs – specialists in the maturing of cheeses – were at other stalls where there was also wine for sale, acknowledging that the two are as indivisible as bread and butter. Elsewhere were the dried fruit; the *vente de haricots de cassoulet* and all the rest of that tribe; the breads, the spices and the herbs spread around us from aisle to aisle. By twelve most of the traders were starting to pack up; a clot

of drinkers, like bluebottles, were still buzzing round the bar and a few customers were making their last purchases. It was time for lunch.

Upstairs, along one length of the building, were twelve bistros. They weren't divided other than by their paintwork, their menus and their smells. Wooden chairs and shiny plastic-coated tables ran down one side, and opposite were the galleys, open, so that walking the length of the room it was possible to see what was cooking – at one the cook was kneading dough on a board on the floor – and to read the menus and the *plats du jour* written up on the blackboards. The prices generally were fifty-five francs for a three-course meal including wine. Paper napkins, carafes of wine and bread were already in place when we arrived, just in time as the room was filling rapidly. Each place had its own revealing or obscure name such as Le

Boeuf or Le Magret; Chez JoJo, Le Louchebem, L'Impériale and Chez
Attila. We chose the Méditerranée at one end of the room because we
couldn't resist its wall of vertical split logs glossily painted a nautical
blue, nor its fishy smell or the beauty of a dish, the shape of a dhow,
filled with oysters. Two women were in the kitchen cooking at a rate
of knots in a space no larger than a loosebox. They had a small oven
at one end and a gas hob at the other. There was one waitress. She
was friendly and brisk, writing our order on a slip of paper that she
pinned on a board beside the cooks. Some of the food, once cooked,
was covered with foil and whisked away downstairs presumably to
the late traders who hadn't packed up yet.

We could see the *merlan* – whiting – coming to the next table in the
traditional way, with their tails curled round into their mouths. While
we ate mussels and sardines David, who was eating tunny grilled *à la
Sicilienne* with rice timbale and red peppers grilled to a sticky brown
with tomato sauce, announced; 'Every multi-storey should have a
place like this.' Amen to that. By now a tunnel of blue smoke and
steam obliterated the far end of the room; decibels were rising, and a
queue was forming on the stairs. It was 12.30.

Into this walked a loose-limbed busker, tall and shambling. He
stood in the aisle beside us and, accompanying himself on the guitar,
began to sing. What rhapsody. Everyone smiled. I hadn't heard the
guttural, vernacular voice of Georges Brassens' ballads for years. To
hear again those well-remembered songs – 'Une jolie fleur', 'Le petit
cheval' and 'Les sabots d'Hélène' – was an unforeseen bonus. I asked
the man to sing on, to sing some more, much to the amusement of the
occupants at near-by tables who goggled, smiling with pleasure at an
elderly Englishwoman enthusing over their beloved Brassens. The
busker obliged; he stood beside us singing and passing round his hat
until eventually he moved on, disappearing into a haze of burning fat.

ON THE BORDERS OF QUERCY AND ROUERGUE where the river Aveyron
passes through gorges is the small town of St-Antonin-Noble-
Val. Here is a pink hotel. Pink as petunias, with blue shutters to every
window of its three storeys. The place looks absurdly decorative set

down among buildings of the Middle Ages when merchants built their tall houses roofed with round tiles and the town flourished. So did the hotel once. Now the delightfully-coloured exterior draws the eye with its lollipop pink and promise of a sturdy lunch among the travelling *cognoscenti* from Montauban. We were lucky. We were just in time. There were a few *cognoscenti*, true, but inside it appeared that the

Simon Dorrell.

place was being 'improved'. Three-ply partitions were on their way in, and on the way out were the high-backed wooden chairs with rush seats, the parquet floor made of curiously long wood fillets, and the high windows with iron contraptions to open and close the view on to the square on one side, the dining terrace and river on another. Any moment someone would replace the few remaining ripply handmade panes of glass; the old-fashioned wooden high-chair for travelling babies; the pretty interior door leading from lobby to dining-room. A facelift was due, we could see the signs. Already the ashes in the large fireplace were cold and the vases of golden rod were in need of water.

I won't bother about the meal. What did matter was the pleasure of catching an old hotel/restaurant on the point of being done over and finding a town politically incorrect as far as tourists were concerned: no concession to other languages; no public lavatories; no 'artisan' boutiques; and certainly no fast food or 'Snacks' – in fact not a trace of tourism. The town might have looked like this for the last forty years. Legacies of the past still remain *in situ* even if not in use, such as an ancient iron water stand abandoned from the days when water had to

be drawn from a public source, and an eroding iron sign for an obsolete walnut mill. Next to the smallest of covered markets is a shop called 'Bazar' with an ogee stone doorway and the proprietor's name, Pascal Montagne, written in ghostly letters above gothic windows so dusty it was impossible to make out what the shop once sold. Only some wording on the glass revealed its days of vanished splendour when you could buy *poterie grès*, *caoutchouc* and *création couture*.

Walking past a glimpse of blue washing on a line seen through vines, we stopped on the bridge leading to the Rochers d'Anglers. From here the houses, with their higgledy-piggledy roofs, appeared as cluttered as an Italian town. We departed. Looking back, the pink and blue hotel was precisely reflected on its head in the still water of the Aveyron.

At last the industrial breeding grounds of Toulouse were left behind and we were driving along a serene road bordered by trees towards la Montagne Noire. We were making for Revel – a town which has a remarkably handsome fourteenth-century wooden market hall with a long shallow roof supported on pillars. It stands on the central square. We were looking for another square; smaller and framed with trees, where the unpretentious Hôtel-Restaurant du Midi is situated. Outside, the menu looked favourable: *salade de céleri rave aux queues de langoustines, millefeuille de foie gras et ris de veau, escalope de saumon velouté de bisque*; an assortment of *brebis*, *chèvre* and *vache* cheeses; various *gâteaux* and chocolate puds, and a crunchy almond *croustillant* with cream garnished with *fruits rouges*.

If none of that was tempting, two boxers were. They were lying in the entrance on their backs. Dogs, not men. Insensible to the world, their pallid tummies exposed, paws and legs entwined with their kohl-outlined lips fallen open like unstitched hems, they took no heed of us. Nothing could be less threatening, nothing could appear less animated, and David and Simon were done for. Both being soppy about dogs, and Simon pining for Georgie and Abie at home, he reached down to pet their inert bodies. Punch drunk, they slumbered on.

Restaurant du Midi
Neither of Us Could Add

THE PARENTS OF THE CHEF, Bernard Aymes, had bought the hotel in 1964. His mother, a widow for twelve years, with white hair and a gentle expression, was charmingly garrulous, longing to please and somewhat forgetful. 'My son, who's the chef – went to Switzerland. He travelled everywhere. He travelled on a big boat. It was the . . . *oh merde, je ne sais plus* . . . it was the big boat that's recently been sold to the Americans. *Le Français!* Or is it *Le Prince?* Anyway – he was seventeen. He was a *cuisinier* on the boat.' Madame Aymes comes from Toulouse, her mother came from the Gers and her father had been a *chef de cuisine*. 'But my husband . . . oh, he had nothing . . . nothing to do with cooking.' And as though to explain why, she added, 'He was from Revel! You can imagine how it pleased my father when his grandson, Bernard, became a chef?'

The menu outside had not misled us. The *rillettes de poisson* with aubergine purée and tomato *coulis* were colourfully harmonious, the plates were plain, the white Gaillac wine (there are reds, rosés as well as sparkling varieties), was dry and light. What did curdle the occasion though, was the intrusive behaviour of the waiters. Because there were few diners, three waiters were endlessly circling and eyeing us like hungry sharks. Bored, they watched our every mouthful.

We ended our meal with that classic country pudding from the Orléanais, *tarte tatin*, for which, when you ask for recipes, each cook has his or her own particular formula. I've never found two the same. Ours was served warmed with *chantilly* cream and a trace of lemon among the apples. The equivalent pudding in England would be heavily sugared, disguising any other flavour but sweetness, but the French have an agreeably lighter touch when adding sugar to desserts. Sauces, fruit and chocolate, or meringue and creamy things, are only mildly sweetened so that the underlying flavour still comes through. Even after ending a meal with something like a chocolate 'dumpling', dense as a praline puffball, it's quite possible to face, without wincing, more sweetness such as a plate of the homemade truffles that nowadays often appears with the coffee.

The next morning trying to make up our bill, Madame Aymes was at her wit's end over the addition. She sat in front of the office machinery softly upbraiding herself for getting the total different on each attempt. As I'm as hopeless myself with figures, we faced each

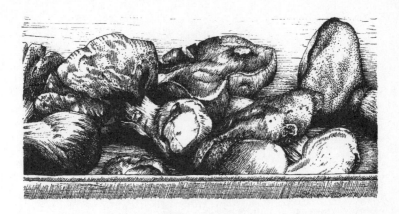

other across the desk for about ten minutes in mutual self-denigration until she called over a waiter to sort us out. She perked up no end when she saw me signing with my left hand. Turning to the waiter she exclaimed, 'Look! Left hand!' When I returned the slip back to her she stared, astonished' *'Voyez! Ça marche, quand même!'*

On Sundays the woods of la Montagne Noire, at the extreme south-west of the Massif Central, are filled with families of mushroom hunters. Their cars are everywhere. With the boots open you can see baskets of every variety of fungi being tipped on to cloths at the back. They gather more produce than any family could reasonably eat, so I imagine they supply restaurants and markets in the neighbour-hood. If we'd had time I would have joined them. I would like to have learnt about the varieties and to have asked how they cooked them at home.

FROM THE RIDGE OF LAND that leads to St-Félix-Lauragais the slopes fall away in treeless undulations. When the maize and sunflowers have been harvested they leave fields of sallow rollers bleached on their crests and darkening in the folds. Sunflowers must do well in this exposed space open to the sky of the Grand Pyrénées Roussillon. They are flowers that as a child I always hoped to catch, but never did,

turning towards the sunrise after waking from their westerly sleep. There are no hedges dividing the crops. The sweeps of tilled earth, stretching to the horizon, become momentarily shadowy from passing clouds. You can see for miles.

The village has a massive church on its summit; a market hall with a beamed roof to die for; a circular tower and a *place* surrounded by tall houses, a few shops and a café-restaurant. More houses with rusty iron balconies and long first-floor windows clutter the hill, giving the village a certain gravity. It also has the Auberge du Poids Public on the outskirts, at the junction of a little road to the left by-passing the village. Here anyone could officially weigh their merchandise, *n'importe quelle transaction* they were undertaking – hence its name.

Auberge du Poids Public
Why Not a Menu of Vegetables?

Among the flower pots at the entrance to the hotel is a remarkable collection of 'sculptures' that are in no way in sync with the *cuisine*. Don't take a second look, walk in. Remember, there's no connection between French decorative taste and that of the palate.

Mushrooms, mushrooms, mushrooms. Once again these magical things were the overpowering ingredient in another chef's cooking. It's hard for us to imagine what it must be like to have to face another day distraught with indecision over what to do with Claude Taffarello's abundance of '*cèpes, trompettes de la mort, pieds de moutons, girolles, chanterelles, pieds bleu . . .* and others I can't remember'. He hesitated. 'We manage to have about fifteen different sorts here during the season. *Coulemelles* or *St Michels* – you know – it's the one found in the meadows . . . a large mushroom.' I didn't of course. My only experience of a profligacy of fungi was picking field mushrooms by the bucketful one August in County Cork. 'People come to the Black Mountains to gather mushrooms. Young people – they bring them here and I buy some. Every Sunday we have a lot of people from Toulouse.' In the spring are there *morelles* in the Black Mountains? '*Bien sûr!*' he said, giving me an indulgent look for asking such a naive question.

MENU TOUT LÉGUME
Vinaigrette de poivrons grillés aux asperges
Artichauts violets cuits en barigoule
Compote de fèves nouvelles
Gratin de fruits frais et d'amandes

Taffarello has the most delicious vegetarian menus. This is one he made last spring. When faced by our pleasure and surprise at such an unusual menu to find in France, he denied it was done to satisfy non-meat eaters. 'It isn't meant in the vegetarian sense! I'm agreeable to vegetarianism – but it's not for that reason – I just adore working with vegetables!' Not enough importance is given to vegetable eating, he believes. 'People in their homes nowadays don't allow time for cooking vegetables. For me they've so much colour, so much flavour!' All through the year he has one menu consisting entirely of seasonal vegetables: piquant, aromatic and an example of subtle eating without the inclusion of fish, fowl or meat. 'It's not usual, I agree – but I'm not unique!'

Beginning his apprenticeship in the *auberge* in 1971 at the age of fifteen ('I'm originally from this region – all my family are here') Taffarello left to travel in the north of France, and then went to Holland and Germany. His wife works at *l'accueil*, in reception, which had been her profession when they first met in Luxembourg. For eleven years they lived on the Côte d'Azur where chefs were trained to cook in the classic tradition.

'I was lucky – my own basis has remained with the old kind of cooking since then, although I did meet Italians working there and we exchanged many ideas and all that.' The flavour of Italy comes into his cooking in many ways. 'Often on the menu there'll be basil, fresh pasta and things with olive oil – Mediterranean cooking – you know. I love it! I wanted to stay on there for ever – anywhere between Nice, Cannes, Antibes and Juan-les-Pins!' Unfortunately it didn't work out financially, so when the proprietor at St-Félix retired, Taffarello, at the age of thirty-four, returned, bringing his devoted head waiter with him. He said quite happily, 'You see, in the end I came back to where I started from.' And regrets? 'None at all. I'm pleased. There's

no sea – but it doesn't matter.' He hesitated. 'Well, it's more authentic here, isn't it?'

The dining-room at the Auberge du Poids Public is large, 'rustic' and dominated in the centre by an old-fashioned gramophone with a speaker in the shape of a gargantuan blue morning glory. Windows on one side look out on to the wide landscape, and round the walls, high up, is a shelf with a collection of farmhouse cookery ware. The Taffarellos are collectors. In a glass-fronted bookcase is a complete set of *Michelin Guides*, starting in 1900.

'They are rare – very rare,' Taffarello told us. 'I began by buying two or three and – well – that was the beginning. I have a thing about collecting. I placed advertisements in specialist journals to get a complete series. Not many people have one. It's not easy!' The first *Michelin Guides* weren't about restaurants, they were handed out free as publicity for tyres and as manuals listing garages for the motorist. In the early editions there are fine steel engravings and a map tucked in at the back. In 1906 the book grew to its present dimensions, though it was not so fat as it is today. 'In 1900 there weren't many garages, so hotels were added and later the restaurants.' The stars began in 1930.

To get a star next year is Claude Taffarello's ambition. 'Yes, of course it's a goal. For us, for the establishment, for the team – it's important. But it's difficult! You have to do the work equivalent of two stars, to get one. I won't do that! *Beaucoup de restaurants, pour avoir une étoile, font un maximum et font le travail de deux.*' Many restaurants, so as to receive one star, push themselves to the maximum and do the work equivalent to a two-star. 'Whereas me, I would be very happy, very pleased to have a star for the work of a one-star establishment!' They are inspected about every two years by a Michelin representative from Paris. 'It's a serious matter. He visits anonymously. He may or may not reveal himself at the moment of departure, when paying.' Surely, by then, it's better not to be told! 'It's crucial there are no problems.' He made a mocking gesture of hopelessness: 'That's why it's a long process! We've been five years working for this.' He sighed. 'Perhaps next March – *dites une petite prière* – we must cross our fingers – *c'est tout!*'

IT WAS SUNDAY AND EVERY TABLE WAS FILLED with French people; family groups, couples, and at one, a party celebrating with champagne throughout the meal with the women in a row along one side, the men along the other. 'Have you noticed that, when a couple come in, the man always sits looking out into the room and the woman sits facing the wall?' David asked. We hadn't; but wondered whether the

men wanted to eye the field or were afraid that their partners might. Dishes passing by, each looking more delectable than the last, left me groaning with longing to try them all: fried whitebait and mayonnaise with tarragon and finely-chopped chives looked fragile and would take up no room; *soupe de poissons et les croûtons avec la rouille* looked thick and would certainly be filling. Sweet peppers and a terrine of aubergines were the colours of soft fruits; red mullet with sesame lay on a bed of tiny diced vegetables; a *gigot d'agneau* from the Pyrenees was carried past trailing wafts of garlic. And *lièvre*: the hare – instead of having been well hung and served in a sauce made from its blood and tasting on the edge of putrid – was freshly cooked, sliced in a wine sauce black as bitter chocolate with persimmon seeds and mushrooms. A scoop of potatoes was crowned by cranberries.

I haven't even started on the puddings.

But we had to try Taffarello's vegetable menu. The produce he adored. Yet none of us had expected the highly-seasoned coco-bean soup with cream to be quite so smoothly and deliciously flavoured. Served with homemade rolls and butter it was perfect. The influence of Provence was apparent in the next course: ratatouille between maize flour pancakes – gooey on the inside, crispy on the top – preceded china bowls with lids in which artichoke hearts and broad beans had been cooked in wine. Lastly something so simple, so exquisitely hot and rich: baked apples filled with ground almonds, surrounded by an astringent plum *coulis* and an almond-shell biscuit containing cinnamon ice-cream. That was the vegetarian menu.

Later I asked the chef why no one appeared to eat cheese. It hadn't been on our *menu tout légume* but nor had other people, except for one table, had any. 'It's because in this region – it's a bit difficult – there isn't a typical local cheese. To find prime cheeses one has to go to Roquefort, to the Lot and Garonne, or to *les Pyrénées* at some 200 kilometres away.' Because there isn't a local speciality he doesn't list cheese on the menu. 'Perhaps one day I'll change all that. I'm not against it – I adore cheeses – but on the menu I prefer to offer one extra course. Customers appreciate that, and we have always some cheese for those who don't.' And the soup we had that was so delicious? 'It's simple. Young white haricot beans – *des cocos* – that's the difference, they aren't dried but fresh. They're cooked with a little onion, chicken stock – and then, very simply, mixed with a little cream. *C'est onctueuse.*' Unfortunately we can't get fresh *cocos*, in or out of their pods, in Britain. And it was these which made the soup so deliciously unctuous.

Cheese isn't the only thing that Taffarello has to procure from far away. 'Beef – it's not a good region for beef.' The pastures aren't lush enough, so he gets his beef from Normandy, from all those green orchards and damp herbage that we'd wandered through earlier in the autumn. 'Veal is different! I cook a lot of veal. There's an *appellation* here. The calves are raised by the sea and this is unique in the French Midi. It gives us the chance to have very fine veal. We monitor precisely where it comes from.' His game comes from Alsace.

It was the same answer I'd had from several chefs in other parts when I'd asked where their game came from. How could such a relatively small region as Alsace keep so many *cuisiniers* supplied with pheasants, partridges, woodcocks, and so on, year after year?

His fish soup, Taffarello told me, made with the addition of little green crabs, had a *rouille* sauce from the Côte d'Azur. 'An authentic *rouille* is made of potato.' I suppose I looked surprised. 'Yes, with their skins on – then one adds eggs, garlic, saffron and olive oil – that's the true *rouille*.' I'd always thought it was similar to a mayonnaise but made fiery by the addition of paprika. He must have read my thoughts. 'Very often in restaurants the rouille is simply mayonnaise with *piment*. That's a bastard sauce! The classic sauce of traditional cooking is with potato. Escoffier writes of the true *rouille*.'

Taffarello changes his menu about every two weeks depending on the produce. 'The menus aren't fixed. We'll change this menu Tuesday or Wednesday – there'll be game on it. But I alter the *Carte* about twice a year.' He has four 'boys' working for him and another who is more advanced, besides the *maître d'hôtel* who came with him from the south of France.

We stayed the night in rooms overlooking rollers of bare land. Leaning out in the darkness to fasten back the shutters, held to the wall by little iron figures, I felt we were aloft, the sky was so immense and the country flowed away from the village like an ocean.

Good hotels never let you down at breakfast, at least not over butter and jam. (Coffee is another thing – France seems to have gone to pot over coffee.) Nor do the really humble places. It's the great spread of mediocre hotels in between, the ones we use mostly when travelling in France, which are unforgivably mean, serving up dabs of coloured food in foil misleadingly labelled *abricot* or *fraise*, and those parsimonious packets of butter. Naturally, here at Poids Public, it wasn't like that. A slab of butter lay in a dish beside a bowl of fig jam along with various breads and croissants. Nor was the milk that ubiquitous Long Life stuff which has taken away for ever the enjoyment of breakfasting at cafés *en route* from somewhere to somewhere.

As in other parts of France, we found that a group of chefs had formed an association to prove that good eating isn't confined to a regional capital, in this case, Toulouse. 'In the *département* much is made of the restaurants in Toulouse,' Taffarello explained, 'but what of us? We cook too.' Nine chefs have formed *Les Terrasses Gourmandes – aux portes de Toulouse les restaurants de charme et de campagne*, circling the city at Brial, Pujaudran, Aurignac, Gardouch, Revel, St-Félix, Fonsegrives, Garidech and Villemur. 'Nine is enough. Our plan is to make communal meals – accompanied by appropriate wines. At the moment we're working on one for 16 November based entirely on *Le Pot-au-Feu*.' He added somewhat quizzically, 'I've got my dish in mind, but I can't remember what it is . . . He promised to look it up later.

The first time they cooked communally was in June when they roasted a young ox on the spit. This time it will be different; using recipes that belong more to the frontiers of bourgeois or even peasant cooking. Each person will make their contribution cooked in a pot.

'Tout d'abord une tasse de consommé dans laquelle ont infusé de belles truffes noires réalisé par tous. They'll start by all making a consommé in which a truffle has been infused, then follow with their individual variations:

Tête de cochon – cooked *en roulade* with vegetables.

Une jambonette de poularde de Lauragais avec des tambinambours et une sauce railfort – with Jerusalem artichokes and a horseradish sauce.

Queue de boeuf en crépine – with young turnips and *moutarde de Meaux.*

Jarret de veau – shin of veal – cooked in a stock with white leeks.

Perdrix – partridge – accompanied by a stuffed cabbage.

Then comes a pause for the *faire chabrot* or *faire le chabrol* – an ancient custom of the south-west when wine is poured into the partially-finished soup which, in country districts, was drunk from the plate. This was a well-peppered soup, made by them all, 'with plenty of red wine in it'.

Poitrine de porc with celery hearts, carrots, *des tartines de légumes* and a *gratin* with eggs – in a beef-marrow sauce. 'That's me!' He'd remembered.

'To crown everything, *un foie de canard* poached in a *bouillon de chou* with *gros sel. Ensuite,* simply a potato *poché en robe de chambre* stuffed with Roquefort! The Hotel du Midi at Revel is doing that.' *Pour bien finir ce repas, un pot-au-feu froid de fruits de l'automne, de notre pays.*' An autumn *compote* of fruit – cold *pot au feu*, 'perfumed with spices. *Voilà!*'

We noticed on the list that not one of the courses consisted of only vegetables. Pork and veal had a high profile, fish and lamb didn't feature. Who are the people who come to this feast? 'First we publicize to our *clientèle*, and then to other people who might be interested, as well as the many fans of the new season's Gaillac wine that is launched on the same day.' As he explained, they are all addicts of dishes *du terroir* which have nothing to do with *haute cuisine*, whose classical features face another way.

When we happened to mention to Taffarello that we'd eaten at a bistro above the market in Toulouse, he appeared astounded. 'But where? Which one?' On hearing that we'd gone to Mediterranée, he shook his head. 'Oh, no! Next time you must go to Attila! That's definitely best.' And he bunched together his fingers in a way I thought only a ham actor did when trying to play the part of a Frenchman. This was for real. Kissing his fingers to indicate what a slap-up meal he'd had, he declared, '*C'est un vrai régale!*'

Recipes

Quasi de Veau du Lauragais Juste Rôti
Roast Veal with Garlic

THE QUASI IS A CUT OF MEAT from the upper part of the leg of veal. It is roasted in the oven with plenty of garlic, one of the staple ingredients of the cooking of south-west France, and served with a *gratin* of potatoes and onions. The recipe, according to Claude Taffarello at *Auberge du Poids Public*, is simple!

SERVES 4

600 g/1¼–1½ lb leg piece of veal, trimmed
groundnut oil for cooking
1 shallot, peeled and finely chopped
12 cloves garlic
FOR THE GRATIN:
100 g/4 oz/1 cup onions, peeled and sliced
400 g/14 oz potatoes, peeled
salt and pepper
stock

HEAT THE OVEN to 180°C/350°F/Gas Mark 4. For the gratin, gently cook the onions in a little oil. Meanwhile, cut the potatoes into thin rounds. Place the onions and potatoes in a gratin dish, then season and pour over a little stock. Cook in the oven for about 1½ hours.

Meanwhile, cut the veal into four equal portions. Tie each piece with string, then brown the veal in a little oil in a roasting pan. Add the shallot, garlic and 500 ml/18 fl oz/2¼ cups water. Increase the oven temperature to 200°C/400°F/Gas Mark 6 and roast the veal above the potatoes for about 20 minutes. Take the meat out of the oven and leave to rest for 10 minutes in a warm place. Remove the garlic from the roasting pan and reserve, then reduce the juices and strain.

Place the potatoes in the middle of a serving dish. Carve the veal into slices and lay the slices around the potatoes. Add the cloves of garlic and sprinkle with the sauce.

GALETTE DE MAIS AVEC LA RATATOUILLE NIÇOISE
RATATOUILLE WITH MAIZE GALETTES

T AFFERELLO LIKES TO SERVE THESE either as a first course or as an accompaniment to *gigot d'agneau*, roast chicken or grilled fish. We had them as a first course on the vegetarian menu and they were delicious. Each one formed a little tower on the plate topped by a maize cap. The contrasting textures were good.

SERVES 8

FOR THE GALETTES:

300 g/11 oz/2¾ cups maize flour, sifted

2 eggs

100 g/4 oz/1 cup wholewheat flour

200 ml/7 fl oz/⅞ cup milk

salt and pepper

50 g/2 oz/⅓ cup raisins

FOR THE RATATOUILLE:

100 g/4 oz/1 cup onion, peeled and diced

olive oil for cooking

200 g/7 oz/1 cup tomatoes, chopped

1 clove garlic, crushed

200 g/7 oz courgettes (zucchini)

200 g/7 oz aubergines (eggplant)

fresh basil

F OR THE GALETTES, in a large mixing bowl combine half the maize flour with the eggs, flour and milk. Season and strain. Add the remaining maize flour and raisins. Set aside.

For the ratatouille, sweat the onion in a little olive oil, adding the chopped tomatoes and garlic. Remove the onion with a slotted spoon. Cut the unpeeled courgettes (zucchini) and aubergines (eggplant) into cubes. Sauté the courgettes (zucchini) in olive oil until they become lighter in colour. Remove the courgettes (zucchini), then cook the aubergines (eggplant). Mix the onion, tomatoes, courgettes (zucchini), aubergines (eggplant) and basil together and cook over a gentle heat for 30 minutes.

Meanwhile, make 16 galettes using small 10 cm/4 in moulds to shape, frying them in a little olive oil and turning them over once.

To finish, for each person lay a galette on a plate, spoon on some ratatouille and cover with another galette.

Gâteau au Noix
Walnut Cake

Makes One 20–23 cm/8–9 in Cake

6 eggs

300 g/11 oz/1 cup plus 6 tbsp sugar

100 g/4 oz/1 cup almonds, chopped

100 g/4 oz/1 cup walnuts, chopped

90 g/3½ oz/scant 1 cup flour

125 g/4½ oz/9 tbsp butter, melted

melted chocolate and walnut halves to decorate

HEAT THE OVEN to 200–225°C/400–425°F/Gas Mark 6–7. Separate the eggs and put the whites aside. Mix the yolks and sugar until they are a pale yellow colour. Add the chopped almonds and walnuts and mix, then stir in the flour and melted butter.

Whisk the egg whites until stiff and fold in gently, taking care the whites do not sink. Grease and lightly flour a 20–23 cm/8–9 in cake mould. Pour in the mixture and bake for approximately 30 minutes.

To finish, pour the melted chocolate over the cake and decorate with walnut halves.

FAIRY-TALE HOUSES AND ICE-COLD MIRABELLE

Alsace

Chapter VII
Alsace

Fairy-Tale Houses and Ice-Cold Mirabelle

ALSACE IS A FOREIGN COUNTRY. So much so that after a time I become homesick for France. And yet its very foreignness is what is so attractive, drawing us back time after time for the architecture, impossible language, fabulous food and the *eau-de-vie* which changes your life for ever. To approach Alsace from the Vosges is a totally different experience to coming at it from across the Rhine when all that flat territory has already numbed the senses with the factories and general ugliness of river industry. But to come to it from the Vosges, from those tumbling hills, from roads snaking down through forests towards the plain: that is something else. And because Alsace is such a small, self-contained area, defined and singular, your arrival is coloured by your first approach.

How you arrive anywhere for the first time is important; primary impressions can never be erased. They may become blurred, confused and slightly out of focus, but the initial impact is unclouded by muddled memories of other times. My recollection of Venice is forever ossified in my mind by arriving there from the sea and walking out of the disembarkation sheds into a crystal-clear light of October along the Zattere; in a book Michael wrote he described our first arrival in Greece as having been by the side door (by car through Yugoslavia), whereas the proper way would have been via Piraeus and to have experienced the Hemlock Moment on the Acropolis. Alas, proper approaches, of whatever kind in life, aren't often achieved, and anyway there's a lot to said for an improper approach in some circumstances.

Above the forests of Vosges lie curious high pastures, the *chaumes*, snow-covered in winter but smothered with alpine pansies in spring and where cows graze in summer among clumps of myrtle. It's believed that in the tenth century bison, aurochs (an extinct species of

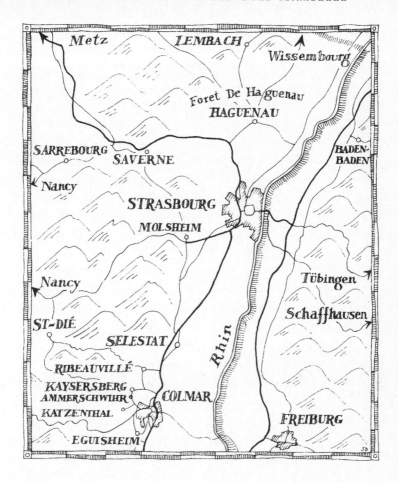

wild ox) and elands roamed these pastures that centuries later were inhabited by a breed of wild horse. Now it's skiers.

The loamy land bordering the Rhine is fertile; it's a giant garden stretching in a broad sweep, parallel to the river on one side and along the foot of the vineyards on the other, rising towards the forests of spruce, fir and Scots pines, relieved by the beauty of beech trees, where game is bountiful. Alsace is famous for game. The *gibier* reaches ovens way beyond the boundaries of the country; Claude Taffarello, as far away as the Grand Pyrénées Roussillon, procures his game from Alsace. Roe deer, chamois (which had to be reintroduced in the upper Vosges hills), wild boar, *lapereau*, young rabbit, and hare (either eaten immediately or hung for three days as Clotilde always did, but never hung until it became high), are on the menus all over France. Pigeon, woodcock, quail, partridge, pheasant, wild duck are among some of the indigenous creatures, though no longer frogs. You may eat them in Alsace, but they're imported, as we had found even in La Dombes, from where the best of France's frogs once came. Crayfish, carp and trout come from lakes and mountain streams, and once the Rhine was rich with eel, bream, pike and carp, but no longer.

The pig reigns supreme; it comes into its own in Alsace and appears in every form from *pâtés* to the ubiquitous *choucroute*. The *charcuteries* are of the best, though we never found one that came up to Émile Zola's description:

> the boned forelegs of ham, with their bonny round faces, yellow with breadcrumbs, and trimmed with a green pom-pom. Then came the great dishes: stuffed tongues from Strasbourg, red, polished, oozing bloody juices, beside the pallid sausages and the pig's trotters, the blood puddings, curled up like pet snakes, the *andouilles* piled up in pairs, bursting with health, the salami, wrapped in foil, looking like choristers in their silver copes, the steaming hot pâtés. . .

Foie gras en croûte is worth pursuing through the miles of menus stuck outside every steep-roofed restaurant, for its truffled interior and rich un-Englishness. Wine flows north to south in an unending spate through names that haunt one's bibulous thoughts when on the threshold of Oddbins: Ribeauvillé, Riquewihr, Mittelwihr, Kaysersberg, Ammerschwihr and Eguisheim. Every village is a stage set offering wine-tasting to your heart's content, and where even geraniums have taken on the herby scent of Gewürztraminer. Wine-making goes on beneath the houses and in handsome buildings surrounding courtyards; so you don't see huge purpose-built hangars stuck out in the countryside. The fruit brandies hoodwink you with their colourless innocence: *quetsche*, *framboise*, *mirabelle*, *kirsch* and *myrtille*. Their distillation of purity has such a fiery thrust it reaches to your eardrums and the soles of your feet in an instant. Each fruit has been transformed into the essence of itself: none more so than *poire William*, the king of *digestifs*. Just to breathe in the fumes rising from a well-iced glass is to recollect those other occasions when happiness was a breath of *eau de-vie*.

I go to Alsace for its foreignness, but unlike other parts of France where we seriously thought of living at one time in our lives, we

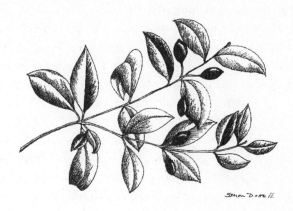

never considered Alsace. Even after numerous visits. It wasn't only because the summer season is torture when the small strip of territory is overrun by visitors oozing between geraniums, but because its quaintness began to make me sick. I'd long for the starkness of the Causse; for the heartland of France, for handsome stone villages that act as a powerful antidote to the pink and red flowery tutus hanging over every Alsatian balcony. Storks (we were *au pays des cigognes*) that nest on chimneys; wrought-iron signs; fountains, timbering and horse troughs full of flowers; pictures of beribboned girls on every plate and tablecloth, all soon lose their winning ways. But come later, come after the *vendange* when the place belongs to itself, and then Alsace is one of the best regions to be, not only for the food but for the darkening cobbles at twilight when the shops shine out on to the narrow lanes, and a single window, improbably high up under the eaves, gleams like a wicked eye tempting you to guess at what's going on up there.

On our way to Alsace Tamsin and I would play games. We'd imagine what we would most like to eat and inappropriately the meal began with fish soup with a *rouille* sauce. Then we'd remember! We were heading east, not to Provence where, when Tamsin was eight months old, Michael and I had first eaten that miraculous, unctuous sauce, so brisk in flavour we remembered it ever after. But now, in the east, would the famous *tarte à l'oignon* be meltingly delicious, with egg yolks and cream saturating the onions lying on a thin layer of *pâte brisée*? Would we find *matelote alsacienne* – a stew of eels in red wine – or steaks of fried carp, brown and crispy on the outside? The agony of conjecture, when we still had miles to go, was too much. We changed subjects.

Anyone who knows Strasbourg will wonder why it doesn't appear in the book – after all, the *choucroute de Strasbourg* is considered the best in France – so although Strasbourg was getting nearer and I had mouth-watering memories of eating *gratin de langouste* at the Crocodile, the beautiful city can't come into this section. It isn't through negligence but lack of time. Strasbourg needs a chapter to itself.

Sit down in a restaurant, peruse the menu, order and wait. If it's your first experience of eating in Alsace, you have over-ordered. The portions are king-size. Unless you have been in training as you meander your way at a slow pace from Calais, you may be defeated at the first meal. I love it. I love this abandoned extravagance that assumes all diners are fit, robust, gutsy eaters in tip-top condition. I also love it that when we turn round and head out of this little slim piece of territory called Alsace, for days afterwards we can live off our fat. There'll be no need to search fruitlessly through guidebooks for a non-existent delectable restaurant at Commercy, Montmirail or Bapaume. *Choucroute garnie* will carry you back to your front door and if you've also eaten almondy *kugelhopf* made with yeast, then Apple Hat and Sussex Pond Pudding will be off your menu for months. My only regret is Nancy. This ravishing city has, among other sights, an unforgettable late-nineteenth-century collection of Émile Gallé's glass at the Musée de l'École de Nancy, as well as the famed splendour of the place Stanislas with gracefully decorative ironwork linking the handsome eighteenth-century buildings. Whether coming or going to Alsace, Nancy has to be included somehow, if only for pure joy; the pleasure of the city works like a glass of Calvados between courses. And the eating there is good too.

T HE RESTAURANT WE WERE GOING TO had not only been recommended by the ebullient chef at Le Gindreau in Périgord, but by Shaun Hill, a most affable chef whose restaurant in Ludlow has undoubtedly upped the eating stakes in that town. On hearing of our journey to Alsace he was enthusiastic: 'Le Caveau at Eguisheim is brilliant. The food's superb.' Unlike the still-born recommendations we'd had in the Lot, this one, as we were about to find out, was very much alive and kicking.

Eguisheim, built around the *château* of the *comtes d'Eguisheim*, is the wine mecca of the district. With a population of about 1,000 inhabitants there are thirty-one *viticulteurs* in the town. '*C'est le berceau du vignoble alsacien.*' The restaurant overlooks the *place* where, on the day we were there, the municipal geraniums were being dismantled by the cartload. At ground level, in '*une atmosphère chaleureuse*', is the *winstub*. On dark wooden chairs under a dark wooden ceiling there's seating for a hundred people among bunches of local flora, a wooden screw from a wine press and barrels built into the wall. It was the first *winstub* to be created in Alsace and intended, originally, to be solely for wine-tasting, but nowadays local specialities are served too. Upstairs a transformation takes place; the character changes. Ten tables laid with white cloths, shiny cutlery and glass create a serene atmosphere in a peaceful setting.

Simon Dorrell.

Le Caveau d'Eguisheim
'JE SUIS TOMBÉ SUR MES PIEDS'

THIS IS HOW A DINER at the next table to ours described how he felt when he first discovered Le Caveau. He's the kind of patron who must be a godsend to a chef: loyal, greedy, extravagant, complimentary, leisurely and overweight. What more can you ask from your punters? Wherever he goes the *maître d'hôtel* instantly realizes that with this one he won't have trouble: here's a well-heeled *gourmand*, and the tip will be generous. So when we sat down at the next table, I could see that a couple of crumpled Englishwomen and a baby weren't exactly in the running. Not that the head waiter flinched for a second; he was the chef's brother and took us on with solicitude, offering to warm Meriel's food and eager to bring a high chair or anything else we needed. This acceptance of infants in restaurants wherever we travelled is heart-warming. Babies and children aren't regarded as unwelcome foreign bodies – oddly, not even by the other customers. Once, in the Morbihan, Tamsin's baby was passed down the restaurant from table to table for the diners to have a therapeutic cuddle between courses. Nor did we come across any place, whether humble or upmarket, where the management made us feel unwelcome, even when the restaurant was full.

Our neighbour – a Swiss with a blonde Sicilian companion – told us how they made elaborate detours to eat at Le Caveau. 'I time my business trips to coincide with lunchtime in Alsace. And this is one of my regular troughs.' He leant over to dab the mouth of Tamsin's daughter with his napkin, in a most uninhibited gesture considering where he came from. Unfazed he continued, 'I can recommend the *bar vapeur et marmelade de fenouil, beurre léger à la fenouillette et oursins*. It's superb! I had it last time.' Although the entry read like consumable poetry – sea bass with puréed fennel and sea urchins – we chose other dishes; but all through our meal, which included *pavé de sandre rôti* circled by frogs' legs cooked in batter and the regional *schifela au raifort*, we surreptitiously kept our eyes on our neighbours, who were having the Menu Dégustation. Each course was

accompanied by the appropriate wine, so obviously the shadow of a breathalizer didn't cast its gloom across their table. The couple kept remarking on the food, sad that we weren't on the same tracks but were suffering from an exiguous and obviously, to them, inadequate meal. When our neighbour had finished the sixth course with its sixth wine and a substantial *kougelhopf en pain perdu*, he turned to Tamsin and said, 'I bet you didn't order this dessert because you thought it would be too like an English pudding!' In a second he'd impaled a piece of the almondy brioche on a fork. 'Here,' he said in such an un-Swiss manner she was quite taken aback, 'have a taste!'

Ordering wine by the glass is usual whether at a *winstub* or a two-star restaurant, and half-bottles are available in most places. The *maître d'hôtel* explained that, because the proprietors of the *caveau* were *viticulteurs*, they aren't allowed to include Burgundy or Bordeaux on the wine list. 'It's a shame but on the whole people prefer to drink the wine of the region,' he said. 'Between eighty to ninety per cent come to drink Alsace wine and those who want a red wine, or something like that, are the *natifs* who are too familiar with our Alsace wine.' (Just as Michel Gomy had found with his oriental food in the Lozère, it was not the tourists, but the locals who ordered it.)

Oliver Nasti, the chef, had worked in England at La Bonne Auberge in Sussex. 'I was young then, nineteen.' Subsequently, before coming here two years ago to take over the concession, he worked under some of the most illustrious chefs: Paul Haeberlin, who reigns supreme at the Auberge de Illhaeusern with five knives and forks and three stars in the *Michelin Guide*; with Jean Schillinger at his two-star restaurant at Colmar, and with Monsieur Roellinger at the two-star Maison de Bricourt at Cancale in Brittany. And yet with all that impressive experience under his belt, Nasti is still only twenty-seven.

With the *choucroute* he offers eight different kinds of meat which he buys from a small *charcutier* at Ingersheim, who is well-known throughout Alsace and who prepares the salt pork that Tamsin had with her *schifela*. Nasti's *cochon du lait* (suckling pig) comes direct from a farm, as does his poultry. 'I never buy meat from the same place – I find what's best. Now there's plenty of game – a lot of venison

– but there's little demand for *marcassin*.' (Wild boar, under six months old.) 'We've tried it, but it doesn't work.' How different from the Ardèche, where appetites for strong cohesive meat, filling and warming, mean wild boar is a much sought-after beast. 'I thought it a very good dish,' said Nasti forlornly. 'We used the *cotelettes* – the best part of the creature – but even so people didn't want it.' However his clientle are mad for venison and partridge.

Pointing to twelve little sacks of spices on a trolley he said, '*J'aime beaucoup ça* – I like using spices very much with venison and game.' Spices are fundamental to Alsace *charcuterie*. He uses all the usual ones including cinnamon, caraway seed, *anis étoile*, ginger and cloves. 'I know the taste and aroma of each one – so if, for example, I'm steaming fish, then I choose a spice that won't be overwhelming. If it's to be roasted, *donc*, I need a spice that marries well with that way of cooking.'

Olivier Nasti is ambitious. 'I became a cook entirely because my mother – she was a good *maman* – was wonderful in the kitchen.' Sundays were important, when the whole family came together for the midday meal. It's of those occasions, he told us, that he had a lot of 'remembers'. For him cooking is always on the move. 'Very simply we're dictated to by the wishes of our customers. Something remains on the menu or it is taken off according to the vagaries of taste.'

Menus, the actual ones you hold in your hand, appear to grow in size every year. Do chefs imagine they are more persuasive on a mega-scale? Are we impressed and cajoled into thinking the larger the menu, the better the food? It's a fallacious assumption. Nasti pointed to the water-colour of Le Caveau on the cover of his fifteen-inch menu. 'It's painted by one of the Haeberlin brothers, Jean-Pierre, who works in the *salle* at Illhaeusern. He paints in his spare time, you know, and he did this for me.'

According to Anthony Blake and Quentin Crewe, who wrote *Great Chefs of France*, Paul, the chef at Illhaeusern, has a kitchen unlike any other belonging to a masterchef. It's more like a domestic kitchen with the staff chattering among themselves, than a 'carefully planned workshop'. Yet it's not to the meritorious restaurants like that at Illhaeusern that Nasti and his girlfriend like to go for a day out, but to where young chefs 'are making a name for themselves because, generally speaking, it's the young ones who have the ideas. Before falling back on to traditional cooking, they have enormous enthusiasm for trying out everything. They're prepared to be adventurous and unconventional.'

THE SPREAD OF GERMANIC APPETITES is catered for in no uncertain terms, and breakfast sets the pace. Oh God, those breakfasts! The variety of rolls, croissants, white, brown and black breads; muesli, yoghurt, plates of paper-thin *charcuterie* and cheese; eggs, bowls of fresh or stewed fruit and jams of such succulent fruitiness, plum, apricot, cherry, wild raspberry, wood strawberries, blackcurrant or blackberry, no one can resist. There's hot chocolate, thickly, richly, darkly, sweetly bitter. It flows down the throat in a hot stream of self-indulgence, but if you can't get through breakfast without your daily 'fix' of good coffee (and it is good in Alsace) then there's always a little tempting mid-morning pick-me-up to be undertaken at one of the pretty cafés in Colmar, where no one sits down to a solitary cup of chocolate without the addition of *pain d'épice* or a brioche oozing almond paste, and where every delicacy is covered with a snowfall of icing sugar.

Walk into the Salon de Thé in Colmar at any time of the day, to discover just how abroad you are. The tea room, where you can eat snails cooked *à l'alsacienne* with wine, stock, shallots, butter and parsley, but no cream, is painted shell pink. How improbable. It's unlike any tea shop I know. Here you're invited to *Degustez à toutes heures nos quiches lorraines* or *tarte à l'oignon;* or, instead of drinking coffee with the cakes or croissants, to try their *apéritif maison, Kir au Gewürz*. The language surrounding us was confusing. We were told that children learn French in school, German or English as their second language and, at home among the family, they use the Alsatian dialect. The waiter was switching from one to the other with seamless fluency. We heard him effusively thanking a young woman in French for delivering something to the shop: 'You are a cream puff!' he declared with passion.

Gradually the Germanic appetite for noodles has become diluted; they aren't as commonplace as they used to be – certainly not the kind when a raw egg in a half-shell sat on the summit of the pasta – those mounds of *nouilles*, invariably tasteless and unaesthetically slithery. They've been replaced by excellent potatoes cooked in a variety of traditionally Alsatian ways such as with scraps of smoked bacon added, or puréed with fennel and *crème fraîche* or as a salad with a little stock, a little cream, and chives.

The gamut of cookery is limitless from a robust peasanty dish such as a potato *galette* – crispy, nourishing and delicious as we had it one night at a *winstub* – to a delicate *vacherin glacé* where the meringue is so light it fragments on the tongue. *Schifela* is smoked shoulder of pork with vegetables and horseradish sauce; *baeckeoffe*, another far from timid dish, is made from beef, pork and mutton, onions and herbs with a liberal dousing of dry white wine which dissolves everything into a harmonious *mélange*. Cooked in an earthenware pot in the oven, it's known as a 'baker's stew'. But most acclaimed, besides *quiche Lorraine*, is *choucroute*, and for details of what the locals do with cabbages read Quentin Crewe's description in *Foods from France*. He tells you everything about the production of *choucroute*, and concludes 'that all products are at their best in their region of origin'. Some might say 'and there they should stay', but Quentin Crewe admits that in Alsace he 'came to see the point of *choucroute*'. Known in Germany as *sauerkraut*, the shredded cabbage is packed into containers and left to ferment. Often served with a separate tureen of puréed peas, the classic accompaniments are bacon, pork and sausages, but there are countless additions and variations according to the cook and what's around. Some add Riesling, some use Chablis, some champagne and others a dash of Kirsch, but when I read what at first I thought must be a misprint, the last-minute addition of truffles, it looked like a case of *auto-da-fé*. Imagine!

The number of gastronomic festivals in Alsace makes exhaustive reading. If they are indicative of the soul of the province, then Alsatians' essential spirit is located below the waist. There are *fêtes* for snails; fried carp; asparagus; cream cheese; *fromage blanc*; *pâté en*

croûte; *pinot noir*; almonds; cockerels; gingerbreads; new wine and *choucroute*; and so on. Those are just some of them. I haven't yet discovered a horseradish festival. Considering how often *raifort* appears on a menu, surely, somewhere, there must be a jolly occasion to glorify the root?

If you are fortunate, as we once were, to be in Alsace in December there's a charming, lightweight Christmas market at Kaysersberg which is all candles and pantomime sets; coloured baubles, tinselly decorations and wooden toys; spice and gingerbread biscuits in the shape of animals, stars and St Nicholas. Nothing is ugly, nothing tawdry, it's a Christmas market out of a fairy-tale with candles in the windows and decorations of greenery along balconies.

The Lion d'Or is at Kaysersberg. Arrive at lunchtime and you will eat in a bustling atmosphere, where there are bowls of oysters and *pinot gris* in a jug. If you're ravenous order the *choucroute à l'alsacienne* which is either cooked in white wine with *lard fumé*, sausages and so on, or there's a version with various fish, including salmon. The dishes are left on your table in an improbably generous heap, enough to feed a whole family. Our waitress, between attending to other tables, kept returning to explain how everything was cooked. For those feeling fragile there's *lard fumé* (a fatty piece of thick bacon) cooked with carp or a savoury smoked fish in a wine and fish-bone stock with a piece of *col fumé*. When it came to the highly smelly Munster cheese, Tamsin and I were hopeless; we hadn't room, nor for *crêpes à l'alsacienne*, but frugally chose *café l'alsacienne* that turned out to be a mere trifle, strong coffee, *marc de Gewürz* crowned by *chantilly* cream.

There are more restaurants in Alsace open on a Monday than in any other part of France. Mondays, which often start on Sunday evenings, are usually desperate days for travellers confronted by a faceless closure from one end of France to the other. Unless you've planned your journey by assiduously searching through guidebooks, you may end up in some fairly scruffy refuge. But not in Alsace. Here everything is sunny. With care you can dovetail your sleeping and eating to be a harmonious and feasting event, for which we have to give heartfelt thanks to the German, Swiss, Dutch and Belgian weekenders. With their bottomless purses and appetites such revenue from across the water (the Rhine in this case) can't be ignored. Hoteliers don't shut on Mondays. There are snares, however. On public holidays in neighbouring countries, Mercedes Benz and BMWs cross the frontier in hordes, descending on Alsace like cormorants. If you haven't booked beforehand you can't get a table anywhere.

THE PLEASURE OF WINE TASTING was enhanced by the gloom of shadowy barrels, with carved spigots, that caught the light on their upper rims. The cool stillness was in silent contrast to the turbulence of gourmandizing. We were standing in the *cave* under the house belonging to the Meyer-Fonné family where Michael and I had been coming off and on for more than twenty years. Meyer-Fonné is not one of the well-known producers; it has about twenty-one acres not many miles from Colmar, on a road that peters out beyond the village of Katzenthal into the rising flanks of the vineyards. Whether the year had been a good one or just mediocre, we always came away with bottles of young and golden wine whose fragrant dryness, drunk on a summer evening in the garden in England, instantly took us back to Alsace.

When the season was particularly fickle, the late harvest (*vendange tardive*), which adds more strength and sweetness to the wine, was ruined. 'The process is a gamble,' Monsieur said. 'Any *viticulteur* around here can try it – all he does is to keep a parcel of land apart, land that has a good exposure to the sun – but it can't be any old vineyard, it must be one that naturally reaches a good maturity.' He handed us each a tulip-shaped glass. 'Try this Riesling, *ça tire un petit peu*. It's a Grand Cru from the slopes around here, cultivated on a particular soil facing south-west.' The Riesling, regarded as the king of Alsatian wines, was clean and granity. 'There aren't any regulations as to how many "parcels" one puts aside, but to achieve the *pourriture noble*, or noble rot – which means the juice in each grape produces a higher level of natural alcohol – there are strict regulations. Nothing is allowed to be added to the wine.' He poured out another Riesling. 'This one's different, you see, *il tapisse la bouche*.' (Literally, it lines the mouth.) 'It's rounder – longer in the taste.' We did our best to get the message. 'A spell of bad weather and all one's business speculation, all one's hopes are ruined. and you can't know beforehand, there's no way of telling,' he said as he began packing up some of the bottles we'd chosen. 'Last year we had no chance of the grapes reaching the right maturity – too much rain.' And he wrote out the bill.

That evening we went to a *winstub*, Les Chevaliers de Malte, in a timbered building the colour of forget-me-nots standing between a rosy-pink house on one side and a sand-washed one on the other. The street was long, the neatness impeccable, and if we hadn't been directed here by a shopkeeper in another village from whom I sometimes buy hand-painted plates with birds or fruit on them, we would never have found the place on our own. Inside, the low-ceilinged room was cosy and crowded. Nine tables covered with red-checked cotton tablecloths, paper mats and cruets were lit by candlelight. Along the bar, sitting on stools, people were already drinking. The *winstub* was for *habitués*, it was their local, where workers dropped in on their way home to drink, to eat perhaps, and leave; the turnover was rapid. By 6.30 people were already waiting for a table and at weekends you haven't a hope of one after 7.00 pm. Several generations of the same family have run the *winstub*; at present it was a mother and son who were cooking, pouring drinks and serving at table.

At one table, a group of diners was sitting round a bowl of 'vine-growers' salad' where the ample slices of ham and salami lay like slabs on top of greenery, hard-boiled eggs and goodness knows what else. We had *harengs marinés à la crème* coiled on to chopped apples, shallots and peppercorns, and served in a white tureen with a lid. Our individual *galettes de pommes de terre* had been pressed down so hard into the pan that they were compacted, crisp and still hissing. We drank full-bodied *Pinot Gris* from tall frosted glasses with green stems, and finished the meal with ice-cream drenched with spirits from a choice of bottles: Kirsch, Framboise, Poire William, Marc de Gewürztraminer or Crème de Myrtilles. The meal was quick and lightweight and just what we needed, having eaten so well at lunchtime in Eguisheim.

Auberge du Cheval Blanc
IT IS THE WORLD THAT HAS CHANGED

'WE'RE LUCKY IN ALSACE. It's the leading region for gastronomic eating at the moment.' Who were we to argue? Fernand Mischler is not to be sneezed at. He's a lion in the jungle of good eating places in this province, where illustrious chefs are as numerous as *villages fleuris*.

'He's a very kind man,' Olivier Nasti at Eguisheim had told us, speaking about Fernand Mischler, '*c'est une belle maison*'. The Auberge du Cheval Blanc is imposing. Like Le Dauphin in Normandy it had originally been a coaching inn; then a restaurant in the 1700s and in 1804 a second storey had been added, but its name has never changed. In a watercolour called 'Réveil à Lembach' painted in 1793, it's possible to make out the old sign of a prancing white horse. The painting shows the military milling about outside the steeply-roofed house with many *chien assis* windows appearing like Cyclop's eyes out of the tiles.

Lembach is a small village north of Strasbourg and fifteen kilometres from the red sandstone town of Wissembourg on the German border. How could a first-class restaurant fail to have a continuous confluence of punters from Stuttgart and the surrounding country, filling the car park and tables with their affluent appetites? On Sunday at lunchtime the restaurant was full; they certainly didn't need people like us with a baby in tow looking for space even though there were families with children. Yet when we walked up the front steps into reception, where there's an intriguing view straight into the streamlined kitchen, and spoke to Madame behind the desk, who was shaking hands and exchanging *auf Wiedersehens* with departing guests, she couldn't have been more welcoming. We wanted to book for dinner that evening; we were staying at a near-by *auberge* and would she mind if we brought the baby with us? 'Not at all. We welcome them!' With her ramrod posture, her dark hair pulled tightly into a chignon, she looked the epitome of formidable Mesdames, and yet by the gracious way she welcomed us you might have thought she'd been waiting for travellers of our sort. Later we discovered she was the mother of the chef.

What an auspicious start. And we'd come here for the flimsiest of reasons. In May, on a plane, I'd sat next to a businessman returning to Marseille; we got talking about food – as one does when sitting next to a Frenchman – and he had written down a list of restaurants in

Alsace where he liked to eat. The one at Lembach was the grandest on his list. Thank you, *cher monsieur*, I was sorry I wasn't able to reciprocate by giving you recommendations for your next trip to England.

Inside, the place was baronial with an imposing chimney-breast and a fire burning. Silver domes with acorn knobs covered white plates initialled with M. *Foie gras* was couched in a ceramic life-sized duck and the service was flawless. Two boys, looking not much more than ten, opened bottles and ran around doing errands. No doubt we were in the presence of potential chefs who in twenty years' time would be adding to the splendour of Alsatian cuisine. Later Fernand Mischler showed us the kitchen – a laboratory where every move had been thought out, where each area had an invisible frontier dividing fish from meat, pastry from sauces and where copper pans were ranged in size along the wall. Every six months a travelling tinker comes by to re-tin those in need. From out of this smoothly-running power-house comes a steady flow of dishes looking exquisite, but not so embellished that they appear inedible. It's one thing to look at a plate and say, 'Wow, that's pretty', because the patterns are intri-cate, and quite another to say 'Wow!' because one's gastric juices are whetted.

Filets de rougets et des marennes d'Oleron were arranged with the two fillets of red mullet flanked by oysters poached in white wine (for seven or eight seconds only) and then wrapped in blanched spinach leaves. The red fish and the dark green parcels were laid on a pale yellow sauce made from the residues in the pan in which the fish had been cooked, to which cream and butter had been added. Cooked at the last minute, it was served very hot. With this Mischler advises drinking Riesling.

Suprême de volaille Albuffera (the lake of Albuféra is in Valencia) is chicken breast stuffed with a slice of *foie gras* cooked in butter, and with a cream sauce with a *soupçon* of mustard and a dash of Cognac added. A slice of truffle sits on top and it's served with green beans and *cèpes*. Tokay is the suggested wine.

Medaillons de chevreuil, thick slices from a saddle of venison, are sautéed in butter, deglazed with Cognac and cooked for several hours in a sauce made from bones and a vegetable *mirepoix*, juniper berries, herbs and red wine. Gooseberry jelly and 'fruit' mustard are gently caramelized and deglazed with raspberry vinegar, to which white wine and shallots are added. Chestnuts, bilberries, and a pear cooked in red wine go with the *médallions*. And Mischler suggests the only wine that is possible is either a good Côtes du Rhône or else a Bordeaux.

Les crêpes au kirsch are self-explanatory. Three sugared parcels, stuffed with a spoonful of Italian meringue mixture, creamed butter and Kirsch, are placed on a plate and browned at the last minute with a red-hot *salamandre* (grill, alas, not gadget). At table the pancakes are *flambéed* with more Kirsch and decorated with a bunch of black cherries.

'A RECIPE ISN'T SOMETHING THAT HAS TO REMAIN FIXED,' Fernand Mischler told us as we sat after dinner drinking coffee and eating *petits fours* so ephemeral we hardly noticed their passing. 'You'll have *une coupe de champagne*, won't you?' A goblet? Of champagne? Why, of course. 'Everything must evolve – *c'est ça*. Often the more classical and simpler things are, the better they turn out. But one can also bring imagination to classical cuisine without wanting to revolutionize everything!' How different, Mischler discovered, were the French from the Japanese when he briefly taught at a school in Osaka. Although more receptive than Europeans, he found that their natural obedience and conformity were death to imagination. 'And I realized how I'd shocked them when I said they should adapt – that products needn't necessarily be married in the same way every time.' 'Intelligence' and 'imagination' are Mischler's culinary gods. '*Plus de fantaisie, quand même!*'

To quench his curiosity as a young man, he'd travelled through Burgundy, the Savoie, Provence and Normandy, searching for their regional recipes. 'One must know a little about all the different regions – especially since I want to preserve French cuisine. I've never been anywhere without bringing something back – I even did from Japan.'

What about in homes; is cooking there slowly dying? 'Perhaps! The problems in the home are international. It's the world that has changed. Now the wife goes out to work as well as the husband and – there you are – who has time to cook?' Even so, some do. Every year Alsace turns out 400 young chefs. They disperse themselves like fieldfares throughout the country – a good many go to the Côte d'Azur as the obvious place – some go abroad, and some remain in the Vosges. We were continually being told that anywhere you go, in towns or villages in Alsace, you eat well. Tamsin and I hadn't yet had an indifferent meal and this goes on throughout the year, November, January and February included.

Fernand Mischler has been training chefs for twenty-eight years. 'I've always got young trainees – when they leave they're as good as I am – perhaps better. And that's ideal!' he said disarmingly. Chefs are no worse than before. 'If they are, whether in France, England or anywhere, it's not the fault of the young but of the older generation!'

In winter Mischler holds classes for men and women who want to learn how to cook, how to entertain. '*Et il y a des fanatiques de ça!*' Many of them are passionate cooks. But what is going on in the less populated regions? What of the Creuse or the Dauphiné? What happens in places where traditional peasant cooking disintegrates into mediocre convenience food? 'Even in the less gastronomically

important departments there still exists integrity. Travel around France! You may find the same ingredients, *foie gras*, for example, in the south, in the west, across the Périgord, *là c'est tout la culture de canard et de l'oie* – but it's different to ours. Different to Alsace.' He was on a high, enthusiastic and confident that we should understand. 'It's this which constitutes the beauty of French cooking!'

While acknowledging the supremacy of Lyon: '*Bon, le Lyonnais, c'est spéciale* – it's different. Everything is concentrated in a small area round Lyon,' (echoes of the lonely voice of Paul Debreuil in the Dombes: 'over there is Lyon with three stars – I'm on my own here'), Mischler is ardently partisan about Alsace. 'You can always find good places to eat – in little villages – anywhere. It's our culture!' Fifteen years ago, he stressed, the *cuisine du terroir* was ignored. 'Of course we have to be guided by our clientèle – everything is evolving – but it wasn't possible in a gastronomic restaurant to serve simple dishes like *saucisses de pomme de terre avec de la viande*. If I'd done that twenty years ago I would have been strongly criticized, whereas today, with a return to the past, it can become a dish in its own right. We should remember this.'

Does he use old recipe books? 'Yes, nineteenth-century books – I used to refer to them much more than I do nowadays. For instance, today one talks of *des huîtres chaudes* . . . ten years ago warm oysters were something out of the ordinary, yet 100 years ago one ate them all the time. Fried or cooked *au gratin*. Not many people know that.' It was the Parisians who started the fashion for raw oysters when bars began to proliferate. 'Now, people are returning to warm oysters, but in a modern way.'

Before we left we asked him for a recipe he particularly liked cooking. 'Yes, I'll give you a local recipe, *une recette du terroir – noisettes de chevreuil* or something like that. I'll have it typed out – the computer and I don't get along. Computers are for the young!' I said one can't be good at everything. He said, 'There are a lot of nice people in England. *Des gens sympathiques* and,' he added with a grin, 'there are a lot of little houses with a lot of little gardens.'

F INDING PLACES TO STAY IN ALSACE, at least out of season, is no problem. Every village appears to have one eating house and every village has at least one hotel or *auberge* frilled up to the eaves with geraniums and hanging signs and seductive menus. The Hotel Heimbach, where we stayed at Lembach only a few hundred yards from the restaurant, was one of those cosy, all-wooden interiors which abound in Austria and Bavaria. They exude homely comfort without having the irritable grandeur that often goes with such good plumbing, linen and central heating as here. We slept under snow-white duvets, the sort you get in mountain country, filled with down. From the window we looked on to a brook running through a village of spotless cleanliness, where housewives shook bedding out of the window and gossiped quietly at their gates. The serenity was palpable. Could life really be like this? And, if it was, how long could one endure it before suffocating under a duvet of complacency? However, as far as Tamsin, Meriel and I were concerned it was a soothing interlude of utter peace.

Another night we stayed at L'Arbre Vert in Ammerschwihr – no, we didn't go to eat at the famous restaurant, Aux Armes de France (now reduced to one star in the *Michelin Guide*) where, many years ago, Elizabeth David described her dinner with glowing intemperance. In a large wooden-panelled dining-room (the village had been destroyed in the war) we ate *rascasse à la Provençale* with tomatoes, anchovies and herbs, and a *sole meunière* cooked in unsalted butter, tasting so fresh and exquisite in this land-locked part of France, that Tamsin said she could smell the sea rising from her plate. The sole lay in pure innocence, unadorned by anything other than slices of lemon. The fish actually came from Rungis, in Paris, the chef told us. 'It takes six hours to reach the kitchen along the wonderful network of roads we have.' We drank Riesling served in a carafe. How pleasant to find that wherever you go in Alsace, you can drink well at a reasonable price; there's no hard sell, no wine waiter hovering while you look through lists of overpriced wine as in other parts of France. L'Arbre Vert has been in the family for thirty years; the wife of the chef is front-of-house, most of the clientèle are *habitués*, and the waiter is Italian. He was born in Eguisheim and used to work at Le Caveau when it belonged to Roger Vonderscher, but when the present owners came the waiter left. 'It hurts my heart still.'

The last thing you expect to see announced in the villages of Alsace is '*Le Beaujolais Primeur est Arrivé*'. Is there no getting away from it? The annual hype even reaches where I live, 'the country for easy livers' (style, not organs) in Housman territory, on the edge of Wales. In our pubs the grand event is written up on blackboards or advertised on fancy cards in restaurants, but is it worth it? I suppose in Alsace, awash with white wine, Beaujolais Nouveau is an exotic ambrosia coming from the granite hills and golden villages of the distant Rhône. Everything is relative. When Tokay is old hat, what joy to drink the sprightly new and garnet-red Beaujolais in mid-November? And in the *winstub* where we'd gone to have lunch we noticed several people, French not foreigners, drinking Beaujolais Nouveau.

The Winstub Zum Pfifferhüs in Ribeauvillé (named after fife players of the Middle Ages) had been recommended by the chef, hundreds of miles away, at Le Gindreau in the Lot. 'It's the best,' he told us, 'Françoise and Laurent are friends of mine – tell them. But get there early – it fills up with locals in no time.' His advice was invaluable. We'd hardly been seated just inside the door when the eight tables were filled and people were crowding the far end of the room and stoically drinking as they waited for a table. Among the lace curtains, the gentle lighting – which should never be underestimated for its effect on the souls of those dining – the dark wood ceiling and walls, the bunches of dried grasses and herbs that hung so low they almost brushed one's

head, the atmosphere was good. It was the kind of crowded, convivial place where the bustle, the chatter and clatter of eating and the smells of cooking whetted the appetite the moment you came through the door. The voracious magic can't be acquired deliberately. The sense of well-being may happen in a *winstub* or in a station buffet; in an Italian *trattoria* or a Greek *taverna*. We have found it in bistros and *brasseries* and most dear to my heart, at Clotilde's on a Sunday. Houses and gardens, though not often enough, also create this third dimension, when you know that, whatever's coming later, you don't want the present to end. So although there were people waiting, Tamsin and I were enjoying ourselves, feeling at ease, warm and relaxed and I wasn't going to think about *haute cuisine* or how the sauce was made.

By the time our food arrived, people were being turned away. A couple of early arrivals who'd been waiting the longest at the end of the room were beginning to sway from either hunger or wine. There was nowhere for them to sit yet they waited with amiably bovine patience, being kept perpendicular by a pillar of coats hanging on the hat stand.

The Alsace specialities included traditional dishes, which never changed, and 'suggestions', which varied according to what was available. Clients have been coming regularly for twenty years, so good and so reliable is the food: black pudding in pastry with apples; braised oxtail; *tarte à l'oignon*; knuckle of pork with *sauerkraut*; *quiche Lorraine*; prunes with Quetsch; Kirsch mousse (made with egg yolks and crème fraîche, and very rich); sherbet with *marc* of Muscat. The grilled black pudding was served with slices of caramelized apple and, instead of mashed potatoes, there was a tile of puff pastry; the *bouche à la Reine* was so generously filled with chicken and mushrooms that little trickles of sauce flowed down the side of the pastry. There were Alsatian sauté potatoes and, blessed of all, a large glass bowl of green salad, the mixed leaves coated in a mustardy dressing. Green salads have vanished;

they've been superseded by such fancy ways of dealing with vegetables that they've often become absurdly outlandish. As we ate among the heightening sounds of eating, ordering, slurping, laughter, sighing and chat, we watched in amazement the endless platters of *choucroute au vin* being delivered to individual diners around us. Cabbage was obviously number one in the charts. You must try it if you go to Alsace, it's good, but we thought once was enough. Could all these people be first-time *choucrouters*? It seemed unlikely: they appeared to be locals, judging by their dialect. We finished our meal with prunes cooked in red wine heavily spiced with cinnamon and aniseed, and then with prunes, coffee ice-cream with *chantilly* and Kirsch. Well, we did want to try everything.

IF I WERE SETTING OUT FOR FRANCE for the first time in my life I wouldn't start with Alsace. But then I wouldn't head for the Mediterranean either: nor the cities. Rather I would choose Burgundy, Normandy or the south-west. I would treat Alsace as a *digestif*, to savour at the end, in winter when the days are short. It would consummate all the journeys that had gone before, leaving me with a good taste in my mouth and a fire in my belly.

RECIPES

LA SALADE DE CHAMPIGNONS DE FÔRET AUX ECREVISSES ET RIS DE VEAU
WILD MUSHROOM SALAD WITH CRAYFISH AND SWEETBREADS

HERE'S FERNAND MISCHLER'S RECIPE - hardly *'une recette du terroir'* as I thought he was giving me!

Mischler uses a selection of four different kinds of wild mushroom, some of which may not be readily available. Make up your own selection and, if only using three different kinds, then increase the quantities accordingly.

SERVES 4

450 g/1 lb calves' sweetbreads

20 freshwater crayfish

light stock or court bouillon

800 g/1¼ lb mixed wild mushrooms, such as girolles, cèpes, trompettes de mort and chanterelles

50 g/2 oz/¼ cup butter

salt and pepper

2 tsp wine vinegar

4 tsp crème fraîche

1 tbsp each finely chopped fresh chives, chervil and tarragon

200 g/7 oz lambs' lettuce

200 g/7 oz oakleaf lettuce

little vinaigrette dressing (see method)

TO BLANCH THE SWEETBREADS, place them in a pan of water, bring to the boil and drain. Allow to cool, then cut into four slices. Cook the crayfish for 2–3 minutes in a light stock or court bouillon. Gently cook the mushrooms in some of the butter and season. Sauté the sweetbread slices in the rest of the butter, allowing 4 minutes each side. Remove and keep warm.

Deglaze the pan with the vinegar. Reduce and stir in the crème fraîche. Then reduce to a syrupy consistency. Season and add the chopped herbs.

Dress the salad leaves with vinaigrette, using groundnut oil, vinegar, salt and pepper. Place some salad in the centre of each plate. Remove the tails from the crayfish and lay four or five around the edge of each plate, placing the mushrooms in between. Gently lay a sweetbread slice on the salad leaves and pour the warmed herb sauce over.

Pommes de Terre aux Oignons et au Lard 'Roïgabrageldi'
Potatoes with Onions and Smoked Bacon

This is a delicious and simple dish to make. In Alsace it is traditionally served with smoked neck of pork and a green salad. It works well with large new potatoes as they retain their shape.

Serves 6
200 g/7 oz smoked bacon rashers (slices)
1.5 kg/3 lb potatoes, peeled and sliced
3 large onions, peeled and sliced
salt and pepper
200 g/7 oz/⅞ cup butter
chopped fresh parsley (optional)

Heat the oven to 200–220°C/400–425°F/Gas Mark 6–7. Line the bottom of a casserole dish with the bacon. Cover with a layer of sliced potatoes, then a layer of sliced onions. Season with salt and pepper. Continue alternating layers of potatoes and onions, adding knobs of butter. Cover the casserole and cook for about 1 hour.

Before serving, thoroughly mix all the ingredients and sprinkle with chopped parsley.

Chapter VIII

IS THERE LIFE AFTER COULIS?

Is There Life after Coulis?

Nyone who cuts a strawberry in half needs help. But on that basis almost every chef is on the verge of cracking up, or so I thought the first time I came across this quite revolting anatomical tonsillectomy arranged on my plate beside halved grapes lying face down in a caramel *coulis*.

Like so many things in life, you can get used to almost anything. I did. Halved strawberries have followed us from one side of France to another at such frequency that I no longer notice these disfigurements of a perfectly fashioned fruit.

There are certain fads, apart from the kinky use of halved strawberries, which affect every region we visited. Other than in simple restaurants, no chef worth his salt would serve a meal unless it was sandwiched between an *amuse-bouche* (or *-gueule*) – which is a form of deliciously edible ornamentation showing off the chef's skill on such a small scale no one can resist these temptations – and a plate of *petits fours* served with the coffee that varied considerably from exquisite to downright leaden. *Cuisine du terroir* is everywhere in the ascendancy and there wasn't a chef who hadn't made that particularly dismissive French grimace, accompanied by an appropriate sound, at the mention of *nouvelle cuisine*. Nor had there been a chef who hadn't at some moment referred to a return to regional cooking and not one of them invented dishes. They might adapt by turning old recipes into something lighter, for *léger* is the current kitchen buzz word. Flowing descriptions of each ingredient on the menu were voluminous, acting not as a stimulant but as a soporific. Supportiveness between the chefs we spoke to was an eye-opener. They were as generous among themselves as gardeners are, with their recommendations for colleagues' restaurants and for acknowledging from whom they had first received a particular recipe. Every dessert comes to table with an intricate lacework pattern of icing sugar squirling round the edge of the plate, and fruit 'soups' and fruit *gratins* are *de rigueur*. Smoking before or during meals is commonplace. And the *café au lait* in hotels is universally dreadful. In an agricultural country it is inexcusable to be given UHT milk at breakfast. Nor is the coffee itself any better; it's either made from the powdered stuff or if it's ground, it's too weak.

Other impressions, fragmented and vivid, come from the pleasure of small things such as a basket of brown eggs in the corner of a *crémerie*; a wooden board worn concave from constant chopping; fingers laying food on a plate with the delicacy of an embroiderer; light shining through a bottle of Tavel Rosé and the slurpy sound of wine-tasting; the intimate sound, like a breath, from a wooden paddle drawing bread from an oven; the design of a gadget used for making patterns in dough; the lettering used for *Spécialité de Pain Campagnard* written across the window of a bakery; the green-grey paint on a fishmonger's shop front; the rustic drawings and words on the paper that's wrapped round *charcuterie*; the lack of food-chain stores unifying to a bland conformity the appearance of every provincial town. And so on, and so on – there are too many of these trivial bonuses to enumerate.

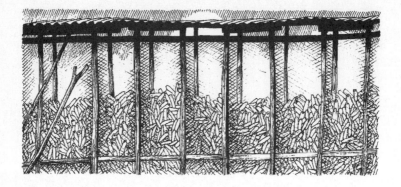

'FRANCE IS AS SHAKEN BY UNCERTAINTIES as any other part of the over-shadowed world.' Those shadows have changed since the 1930s when Ford Madox Ford wrote that. In the 1990s when we set out to find the legendary food of France, I had anticipated a celebration rather than a death-rattle. We found both. There were mornings when I awoke with a weary ferocity from the need to push on; without the certainty of a successful day's eating it was easy to feel sapped before we started.

Years ago, if all else failed, there was always the railway station for good eating even if the surroundings might not be wildly salubrious. In cities you can still find reasonable station food, even if it isn't up to the high class and expensive standard of the Table Train Bleu at the Gare de Lyon in Paris. Andrew Shirley, writing in the late 1950s, said, '. . . if you are well advised you will lunch or dine there [the station] as often as is convenient'. And as though forestalling the reaction of contemporary travellers, he continued, 'This sort of idea is basically repugnant to the Englishman, who knows what happens even to reasonable food once a railway official has even thought about it. But in France . . . they demand serious food at the station.'

How true. Or it used to be. Station food was infallible. Once, at Belfort, a town without a high profile among travellers, which lies between the Vosges and the Jura – a region we were often traversing – we ate an excellent meal at the *gare*. *Feuilleté au fromage*, light as air and brought to the table the moment it was cooked, spearheaded a cartwheel of frogs' legs for the two of us cooked with parsley and butter, followed by *poularde de Bresse au vin jaune* (a wine as yellow as buttercups) in a creamy sauce and with the Gruyère on top still heaving. We ended with a *bavarois aux fruits* made with apricots. But now eating at stations is touch and go; there are excellent meals to be had at certain ones, but you can no longer rely on their trustworthy standards. Friends, who took the train from Hereford and descended at Gourdon in the Lot, found station food throughout the journey abysmally dreary.

Changes for the better have occurred in some ways, though. Eating in French houses used to be distressingly formal; it was far more relaxing to be entertained at an excellent restaurant, especially as one's hosts knew exactly where to go to eat well in their neighbourhood. But the laboured conventions in their homes, their inhibitions, their anxiety as to whether we could eat this or that, was a protracted agony in which everyone felt uneasy. Thank goodness there's been a loosening up of dining conventions. Visitors from France admitted how, with a certain envy, they couldn't get over English casualness, our laid-back attitude and our unperturbed concern over what to them were part of civilized conventions when entertaining. John Ardagh, writing in the 1980s, says:

> And even Parisians, when they get round to it, are now entertaining much less stiffly and ceremoniously than in the old days . . . Most young people, freeing themselves from the formal standards and obligations of their parents, have become far more casual and informal in inviting friends as well as relatives to meals.

If you land in France a culinary virgin, aren't you in luck? You arrive unburdened with all these leftovers of remembered meals; you have no gluttonous yardstick in your baggage; no curdling of the present by comparisons with the past. Had I come to France for the first time in the 1990s how differently this book would have turned out. To start with I would have assumed that 'violet' mustard was the norm; that *aux fruits rouges* was the ubiquitous accompaniment to almost every savoury or sweet course; that slices of meat or game have customarily been fanned out on top of a sea of sauce; and I wouldn't have looked back wistfully to a time when vegetables were more than token decorations to placate the god of calories.

But then nothing is repeated. No meal will turn out to be identical to the last time you ate or cooked it, any more than the garden will be the same as last year. No restaurant will give you the same *frisson* at being there as it did on the first occasion. How boring if cooking were infallible – or gardens, or people – there's time for infallibility in the grave. Cooks know this, and that's why boil-in-bag food has an odious predictability. Every time. Sterility is unromantically dependable. Each of the chefs in the book is worth returning to because, however fired-up you might be to taste what I've written about, what you will eat on that day, at that time, will be her or his creation, unique and like no other. Everything is inimitable.

If I hoped to find Clotildes I realize, like salamanders, how elusive they've become. True, we found her in the Ardèche, we found her in Normandy and in the city of Lyon, and I know of a southern Clotilde whose name has been given to me by one of the chefs. 'She and her husband grow all their own vegetables . . . the cooking, truly...it's wonderful! What's more – one eats for *un prix dérisoire* – a ridiculous price . . . it's given away!' The restaurant is in a village, open only at lunchtime and with about ten tables. 'If you have the chance, go. It's very spontaneous. In the first room you enter there's the bar and the bistro, behind there's another room with a large fireplace in which they also cook. The woman who runs it came twenty-five years ago. Since then she's created . . . ' and he threw up his arms dramatically, gesturing in sign-language just how superb the food is, '*une cuisine!*'

I'll go there one day, and I'll go to the place up a mountain at the back of Marseille where you need a password to cross the threshold. There are other Clotildes too, so remote and obscure, that I've found them hard to locate on the map.

I began by believing in a sprinkling of Clotildes, and I've finished with that belief intact, even though they have become an endangered species under threat of extinction. We're lucky to be living at a time when we can still find them, as we can the country women selling one honeycomb and a few eggs in a market or, moving into another dimension, that we're living at a time when we can still walk the quays of Venice before they submerge under the incoming tide. My grandmother may have been the first woman to ride a penny-farthing in breeches; will my granddaughters be among the last to eat in a kitchen like Clotilde's?

I'VE COME TO THE END OF MY DUAL QUEST for chefs and salamanders. A quest that has been a torment and a revelation. Chefs are available. I'd no idea they'd be so easy to catch. Obviously they're happy people, thriving in their chosen *métier*, and in no hurry to put up the shutters once the last meal is served. They talk about themselves, about food, about France, with the impassioned intensity and jovial good nature of total culinary addicts.

But has the search been successful? As far as salamanders are concerned there's no doubt; the implement sits on my hearth waiting for me to light the fire. After travelling in all directions and plaguing shopkeepers to look among their *batterie de cuisine* for a *salamandre*, how wayward that I should find the implement on our last journey and so near home. In Dieppe. Unfortunately its melodic name, *salamandre*, has gone up in smoke and been replaced by *un fer à caraméliser*. Perhaps if I'd set out asking for a 'caramelizing iron' I might have found one sooner, but then myths are meant to be chased, and travel would lose its piquancy if one wasn't enthralled over something or other. I've also seen pictures of the pretty creature splodged with orange blobs, on film. They have furtive habits as endearing as their smaller relatives, the newts. As for a salamander's *alter ego*, the legendary beast that withstands the flames, it still haunts my imagination with its imagery and tall stories.

Could I say chefs were enthralling? Well, not exactly, but I could say they were lively, dogged, articulate, sanguine and certainly genial. But the reputation for the French having the best food in Europe can't any longer be taken for granted and if ingredients are the basis of all good cuisine, there's absolutely no excuse for a decline in restaurants. Their produce must be the best in Europe. 'We've a lot of schools, we've *un reservoir fantastique* of young chefs who've been trained,' Fernand Mischler reassured us, when I spoke of our forebodings over the way France was going, 'and Alsace even more than Lyon is the leading region for gastronomic eating at the moment.' Although some might dispute this, one thing is certain: not a single chef whom we spoke to was gloomy. Some were more upbeat than others; and where their own particular region had once produced superb fruit or frogs, pork or fish, now they had to contrive to get the ingredients they sought, whether from Rungis or abroad. This was happening to such an extent we had the impression that the whole of Europe was growing each other's indigenous produce. When Claire, of 'Claire's Flying Fish', our local *poissonnier*, and who therefore was in the know, went to Greece recently, she refrained from ordering the famous red mullet – she knew too much – Greece no longer has any red mullet; it now has to be imported from Birmingham, from where it's shipped frozen out to Greece to satisfy tourists' demands for 'local' produce.

I F THERE ARE MOMENTS NOW THAT I'M HOME when I recall how often my resolution wavered, those apprehensions are swiftly overlaid.

Early one morning in autumn Claude Taffarello at the Auberge du Poids Public left his kitchen in the hands of his chef assistant. He was setting out to talk to schoolchildren about the food of France. In a black briefcase he'd packed his chef's hat (normally he never bothers to wear one) and bunches of herbs. In a basket he'd piled fruit and vegetables – a persimmon, pomegranate, squash, green tomatoes, and so on, alongside a large flat country loaf wrapped in a teacloth. In a second basket, laid among bracken, were collections of twelve different types of mushrooms gathered from la Montagne Noire. This wasn't some freaky ploy of his that he'd thought up the night before, but a sweep of imaginative education undertaken by fifty-nine other colleagues of his, who were circling Toulouse with their baskets of food. The children were going to learn of their regional produce, their culinary heritage, and of what epicurean delights can still emerge from a French cuisine.

Addresses of Restaurants

Chez Paul, 11 rue du Major-Martin, Lyon 69001. Tel: 78 28 35 83

Auberge des Chasseurs, Bouligneux 01330. Tel: 74 98 10 02

Le Gindreau, St Médard 46150. Tel: 65 36 22 27 Fax: 65 36 24 54

Au Déjeuner de Sousceyrac, Sousceyrac 46190. Tel: 65 33 00 56 Fax: 65 33 04 37

Les Falaises, Gluges, 46600. Tel: 65 37 33 59 Fax: 65 37 34 19

Au Grand Duquesne, 15 pl. St-Jacques, Dieppe 76200. Tel: 35 84 21 51 Fax: 35 84 29 83

Au Caneton, r. Grande, Orbec 14290. Tel: 31 32 73 32

Le Cheval Blanc, pl. René Coty, Caudebec-en-Caux 74490. Tel: 35 96 21 66

Auberge des Ruines, pl. de la Mairie, Jumièges 76480. Tel: 35 37 24 05

L'Hôtel du Dauphin, pl. Halle, L'Aigle 61300. Tel: 33 84 18 00 Fax: 33 34 09 28

La Mare aux Fées, Villers-Haudricourt 76390. Tel: 35 93 41 79

Panoramic Escrinet, Aubenas 07200. Tel: 75 87 10 11 Fax: 75 87 10 34

Hôtel-Restaurant La Clède, Villefort 48800. Tel: 66 46 80 14 Fax 66 46 85 26

Chez Francine, Montselgues, Les Vans 07140. Tel: 75 36 94 44

Hotel-Restaurant du Midi, 34 bd Gambetta, Revel 31250. Tel: 61 83 50 50 Fax: 61 83 34 74

Auberge du Poids Public, St-Félix-Lauragais 31540. Tel: 61 83 00 20 Fax: 61 83 86 21

Caveau d'Eguisheim, 3 pl. Château St-Léon, Eguisheim 68420. Tel: 89 41 08 89 Fax: 89 23 79 99

Lion d'Or, Kaysersberg 68240. Tel: 89 47 11 16 Fax: 89 47 19 02

Auberge du Cheval Blanc, Lembach 67510. Tel: 88 94 41 86 Fax: 88 94 20 74

L'Arbre Vert, Ammerschwihr 68770. Tel: 89 47 12 23 Fax: 89 78 27 21

Winstub Zum Pfifferhüs, 14 Gd' rue, Ribeauvillé 68150. Tel: 89 73 62 28 Fax: 89 73 80 34

Sadly, since I started writing this book, Clotilde has died. Chez Clotilde exists no more.

BIBLIOGRAPHY

Ardagh, John, *France Today*, Penguin Books, London, 1982

Aron, Jean-Paul, *The Art of Eating in France*, English edition, Harper & Row, London, 1975

Baldick, Robert, *Pages from the Goncourt Journal*, OUP, Oxford, 1962

Bentley, James, *A Guide to the Dordogne*, Viking, 1985; *Life and Food in the Dordogne*, Weidenfeld & Nicolson, London, 1986

Binns, Richard, *Allez France!*, Chiltern House, Leamington Spa, 1994

Blake, Anthony & Quentin Crewe, *Great Chefs of France*, Mitchell Beazley, London, 1978

Chamberlain, Samuel, *Bouquet de France, An Epicurean Tour of the French Provinces*, Gourmet, New York, 1952

Courtine, Robert, *The Hundred Glories of French Cooking*, Farrar, Straus & Giroux, New York, 1971

Crewe, Quentin, *Foods from France*, Ebury Press, London, 1993

David, Elizabeth, *French Provincial Cooking*, Michael Joseph, London, 1960; *English Bread and Yeast Cookery*, Penguin Books, London, 1979

Davidson, Alan and Jane, *Dumas on Food, Recipes and Anecdotes from the classic Grand Dictionnaire de Cuisine*, OUP, Oxford & New York, 1987

Deighton, Len, *ABC of French Food*, Century Hutchinson, London, 1989

Escoffier, A., *A Guide to Modern Cookery*, Heinemann, London, 1907

Grigson, Jane, *The Mushroom Feast*, Penguin Books, 1975

Harris, G., *Pots & Pans*, Penguin Books, London, 1980

Hartley, Dorothy, *Food in England*, Macdonald, London, 1954

Hill, Shaun, *Gidleigh Park Cookery Book*, Century, London, 1990

Johnston, Mireille, *French Cookery Course*, BBC Books, London, 1992

Oyler, Philip, *The Generous Earth*, Penguin Books, London, 1961

Penton, Anne, *Customs and Cookery in the Périgord and Quercy*, David & Charles, Newton Abbot, 1973

Phillips, Roger, *Mushrooms*, Pan, London, 1981

Rance, Patrick, *The French Cheese Book*, Macmillan, London, 1989

Shirley, Andrew, *South from Toulouse*, Scribners, New York, 1959

Strang, Jeanne, *Goose Fat and Garlic, Country Recipes from South-West France*, Kyle Cathie, London, 1993

Tilleray, Brigitte, *The Frenchwoman's Kitchen*, Cassell, London, 1990

Vandyke Price, Pamela, *Eating and Drinking in France Today*, Scribners, New York 1966

White, Freda, *Three Rivers of France*, Faber and Faber, 1952

Index